CHEC

// International Edition

K IN /

Christian van 't Hof
Rinie van Est
Floortje Daemen

Rathenau Institute
NAi Publishers

The Public Space as an Internet of Things

Contents

Foreword

With the rise of the Internet in the mid-1990s, expectations were high. Now, most people are on-line and have a mobile phone. In 2010, the number of Internet users has surpassed two billion, approaching a third of the world's population. Furthermore, there are 5.3 billion mobile phone subscribers; mobile phone networks are already available to over 90 per cent of the world's population, and smart phones are becoming the focal point of the personal communication experience. By 2020, our 'digital universe' (i.e., all data created by consumers and businesses on earth, including video, audio, documents, etc.) will be 44 times bigger than it was in 2009 (i.e., it will expand from 800 *billion* gigabytes to 35 *trillion* gigabytes). Furthermore, the number of 'objects' (i.e., files that contain digital data) will increase faster than the total amount of data, due to smaller file sizes. Thus, even though lots of large video and audio files are being created, so are massive amounts of small files created by devices, sensors, etc.

Does this signify the virtual end of 'Information Society'? 'Information Society' is a term that dates back to 1973 from the book of sociologist Daniel Bell, which became popular 20 years later within the context of the development of the World Wide Web and Information and Communication Technologies, especially after the European Commission report on 'Europe and the Global Information Society' was published in May 1994. 'Information Society' is not coming to a virtual end, because we are entering a new phase: the digitalisation of public places.

This new phase has already become visible in some locations around the world, in particular in Tokyo, Japan, where, since 2007, Professor Ken Sakamura started assigning *ucodes* (128-bit meaningless numbers used as identifiers which are put into computer-readable tags) to objects (e.g. in offices, schools and hospitals) and to locations (e.g. for learning what services are available in the neighbourhood). Today in Europe, local and regional networks such as CEMR/ELANET, eris@, EUROCITIES and Major Cities of Europe are increasingly scaling up their responses to the

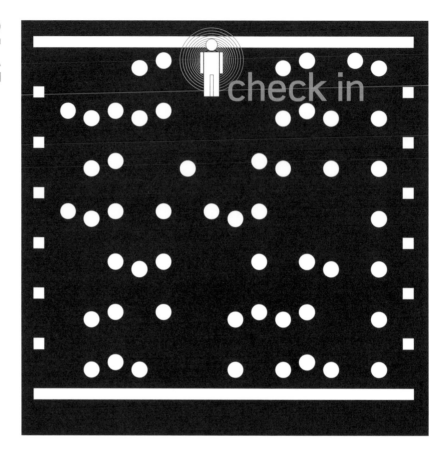

check in

challenge of the Internet of Things and Ubiquitous Networks. As a result, more and more cities, as well as regions and rural areas, are investing in Internet-enabled services, each according to their own style and vision. For example, the Amsterdam Smart City initiative aims at implementing, within a two-year period, fifteen projects in the sustainable focus areas of working, living, mobility and public space.

Now, when we use public transport, drive our car, walk in the streets or enter a building, we continuously 'check in' and 'check out' with different networks. As these networks are increasingly linked, we are continuously on-line. We do not only surf *on* the net, with our PCs and mobile phones – we are actually *living in* the net. The Internet gives: it shows us the way, enables us to pay, provides access, and lets us be known by others. It can empower us. But the Internet also takes: businesses and governments may use it to know our whereabouts and control us. Therefore, our privacy is likely to be infringed upon by the accumulation of personal data that is collected, compiled, analysed, reused, disclosed, and/or sold in unimaginable ways, often without the user's knowledge or consent.

Are empowerment and privacy each other's counterparts? The authors of this book set out to perform a daunting task: to demonstrate that a 'good balance' exists between giving control (privacy) and taking control (empowerment). Such a balance can be achieved by introducing the concept of Identity Management.

I believe that any new contribution to the growing literature on the Internet of Things has to achieve three basic aims. This book fulfils all of these requirements. First, it defines the current 'state of play' by explaining the underlying theory of the subject – from being *on* the net to going *into* the net. Second, it builds a skill base for those who would wish to become seriously involved in the design and/or deployment of useful and effective internet applications – this book does this by referring to five existing cases and by sketching the future scenario of a Living Map. Third, it establishes credence in terms of its usefulness, accuracy and the reliability of its content – the Rathenau Institute is the Dutch office of Technology Assessment, advising the Dutch and European Parliaments on the societal aspects of technological developments.

Perhaps most importantly, like nothing else out there, this book shows us how to grasp the human side of business and technology, and that being human is the only fate from which we can never escape. The Internet of Things will realise its full potential only if it is, first of all, an Internet of People. The Netherlands is a particular case indeed. Some of the world's leading companies are based in the Netherlands: TomTom with their satellite navigation devices, NXP, which supplies RFID chips, and ASML, which provides the silicon wafers for chips. The Dutch are ambitious in being the first country to have all public transport on one smart card. Finally, this country has a tradition of lively debate about the implementation and failure of large IT systems.

It was for me a great honour to be invited to write the foreword to this book. I have worked in the area of the Internet of Things for the past five years and I have come to understand the power, the value and the challenge that it can bring to society. I enjoyed this book immensely and I recommend it to all those who wish to reflect upon this exciting and inspiring area.

You are 'checked in' now. Have a nice journey. But will you be able to 'check out' again?

Gérald Santucci
Head of Unit 'Networked Enterprise and RFID', DG Information Society and Media, European Commission and Acting Chairman of the Expert Group on the Internet of Things

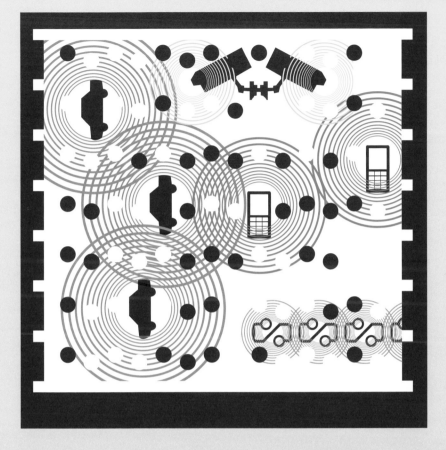

Introduction

Living in the Net

Christian van 't Hof and Rinie van Est

'The net gives and the net takes – and we live in the middle of it all.'

A New Phase in the Information Society

In public space we are increasingly surrounded by digital devices. Cameras guard over our safety, antennas and sensors keep track of our driving speeds, and digital wicket gates determine whether or not we gain access to the train station. Provided with an ever growing arsenal of identification numbers in ID cards, mobile phones and vehicles, we prove who we are, that we have a right to be there, and that we paid for it.

With the growing digitalisation of public space, our information society is moving into a new phase. We do not only *surf* the net from behind our computers; more and more, we are *living in* the net. *Check In / Check Out* examines what this new phase in our information society will mean for citizens. How do new digital technologies enhance user prospects? Are they liberating or might they actually restrict the privacy of citizens? And how do these developments influence our experience of public space? Does the rise of new information technologies cause different power relations? And who are actually behind the network of digital devices that look at us and judge us?

We advance the proposition that digitalisation of public space signifies a new phase in the information society. In the rest of this book we substantiate our proposition based on a few recent developments: contactless smart cards in public transport, CCTV, Near Field Communication, GPS, Google Earth and Street View. We continuously search for the social implications of new, digital techniques in public space. A central concept we make use of is *Identity Management* (IdM). In short, Identity Management brings together two important social preconditions for the application of Information Technology: enablement of individual and collective action (frequently referred to as *empowerment*) and the need for a safeguard for personal privacy.

From Being *on the Net* to Being *in the Net*

At the end of the 1970s it became apparent to many people that society had entered a new era; that of the *information society*.[1] The influence of information technology in factories, banking, medicine and telecommunication, could no longer be denied. In light of high unemployment, automation was regarded with some suspicion.[2] In those times, computers symbolised the power of large corporations and government institutions. The unexpected appearance of *personal* computers, as a product of the counterculture, gave information technology a whole new, positive, and liberating meaning.[3] PCs brought computers into the living room – first for hobbyists, and soon enough, through computer games, also for young people.

We are *on* the net ...

Internet and e-mail became popular over the course of the 1990s. Because of these new applications, PCs became part of a worldwide communication network, the World Wide Web. An old dream came true. As early as the 1930s, writer H. G. Wells fantasised about a *World Brain*, a kind of Wikipedia as we know it now. In his science fiction novel *Neuromancer* from 1984, writer William Gibson launched the term 'cyberspace', which visualised the omnipresence of a virtual world. Nobel Prize winner Al Gore had devoted himself since the 1970s to creating an *Electronic Highway* that brings people together and makes room for new economic possibilities. Apart from 'nerds', this new, virtual world was mostly colonised by young people, the so-called 'digital generation'.[4] Public discussions kept raising the question if internet empowers citizens through faster and better access to information, or if it mostly means a loss of privacy and produces new dangers, such as digital crime.[5]

And we go *into* the net

Today we take our personal computer – in the shape of laptops and smartphones – into public space en masse. This public space itself is also filled with digital devices. Wicket gates can only be opened with digital cards, sensors count people and vehicles, cameras follow us and GPS guides us. At the same time, networks that were once separate are now being merged. Internet, telephone, radio and television are increasingly using Internet Protocol (IP). In this way, the internet is more and more becoming a network of devices that surround us, wherever we are. Like

The majority of citizens are currently on-line.

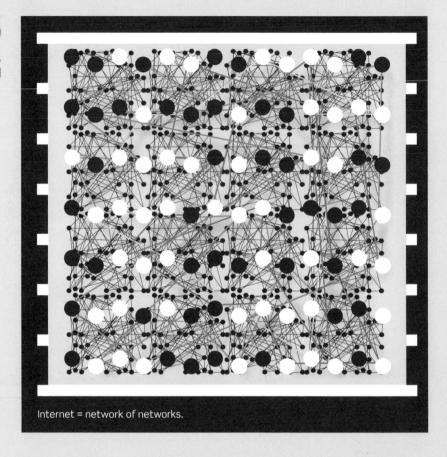

Internet = network of networks.

this, we go from being *on* the net to being *in* the net. The digitalisation of public space marks a new phase in information society. Researchers, companies and authorities in various parts of the world recognise this.

In South Korea and Japan, a so-called *Ubiquitous Network Society*[6] has become the dominant vision of authorities, companies and research institutes. U-Korea and U-Japan are entwined in a fierce competition to be the first country to connect all chips, sensors and other devices to a single network. Governments grant subsidies of billions of Euros for pilot projects that are performed by university laboratories and large corporations such as NTT Do Como and Samsung. The goal is that ever-present, invisible devices are always at a consumer's beck and call. This changes the internet as we know it into a virtual layer on top of our physical reality.

The United States government has not yet set out to create something like U-America, despite the fact that the term Ubiquitous Computing[7] was coined by the American Mark Weiser. Weiser, however, particularly aimed for an automated office environment, without linking to the internet. While large IT companies in the United States develop applications along the trend of getting *in* the net, the government still hasn't shown to have any strategies in this field. Al Gore's notion of the *Information Super Highway* is still dominant. This policy is especially focussed on getting companies and individuals on-line. With regard to fighting terrorism, strict security policies have been integrated. Think of the security programme *Total Information Awareness*, which is about tracking down and following potential suspects. Some individual attempts to point out the digitalisation of public space, such as Adam Greenfield's *Everyware*[8], have not yet lead to governmental shifts in thinking about our information society.

In Europe, like in Southeast Asia, billions of Euros are being invested into researching the development of digital techniques that help users find entertainment, service and security, depending on personal wishes, in both inside and outside spaces. A first concept to coin this development was *Ambient Intelligence*[9], or intelligent environments. This term was introduced in 2001 by Philips and the Information Society and Technology Advisory Group (ISTAG). Another label is The *Internet of Things*, coined by the International Telecommunications Union in 2006.[10] Viewing the numbers of official documents and meetings, it seems this concept is gaining dominance.

The Internet of Things is currently also the dominant concept for information society in China. The Chinese prime minister Wen Joabo announced in 2009 that they will invest 50 billion RMB (5 billion Euros) over the next five years in *Sensing China*.[11]

A technical definition of the net

Ubiquitous Network Society, *The Internet of Things*, Ambient Intelligence or Everyware – all these terms presuppose the emergence of a single network, one that is available everywhere and that connects all devices. They create a lively image of an abundance of technologies without an excessively complex technical explanation, but they do all have historical backgrounds and normative overtones. In this book we bring together technologies under our own term: the net. This net consists of the joining of various networks that connect diverse devices and ascribe unique identification numbers to everything that falls within the net. Within this net, data systems slowly fuse to become a single system to which we are practically always checked in.

Internet is, by definition, a network of networks. It started with a digital signal over analogue telephone lines. The creaky beeps on the line represented packets of zeros and ones, which were supplied with the addresses of the sender and the recipient, the so-called IP (Internet Protocol) addresses. Gradually, more and more wires were added. Physically, these included the coaxial cable for television, glass fibre and even electricity cables; wirelessly, these included Wi-Fi, UMTS, GPRS and WIMAX. You may notice the difference between networks – one channel is faster, more available or cheaper than the other – but for the zeros and ones it doesn't matter which medium is used. They still have to be converted into data, otherwise machines will not understand them. For this, many languages have been developed that increasingly link up with that one universal language: the Internet Protocol.

The networks and whatever happens within them largely remain hidden from us. We mostly see the many devices that are linked to them: smart cards and their readers, laptops, mobile telephones, information screens, antennae, satellite navigation systems and cameras. Next to these, there are many devices in the net that we do not see. Such as the routers between the cables, which use IP addresses to see what data packet needs to go where, also if somewhere along the line something fails to operate. Or the 32 satellites of the Global Positioning System, of which a navigation system needs four in order to determine where it is located (sometimes it is believed that the navigation satellites follow the car, but it is actually the other way around). The RFID (Radio Frequency IDentification) chips, too, stay out of sight, because they are so small. This is because they don't have a battery; they retrieve the energy they need to send out signals from the signals that they receive. Their antennae are simultaneously electromagnetic coils. The most important devices that we do not

see are perhaps the many databases that store all this data: from a tiny computer script somewhere in the network to massive, heavily-guarded data centres.

It is also important that devices are able to identify each other with the use of unique numbers. Computers have an IP address, mobile phones a SIM card and IMEI number, RFID chips have a UPC Global code, and so forth. To illustrate how simple it is for a single number to divulge large amounts of information in the network, this book is provided with matrix codes. These codes are no more than printed zeros and ones which are legible to an optical reader. Within the net, the number refers to a place where data is stored. We chose Microsoft Tags[12] for this book, but there are alternatives such as the black-and-white blocks in QR code[13], or the familiar

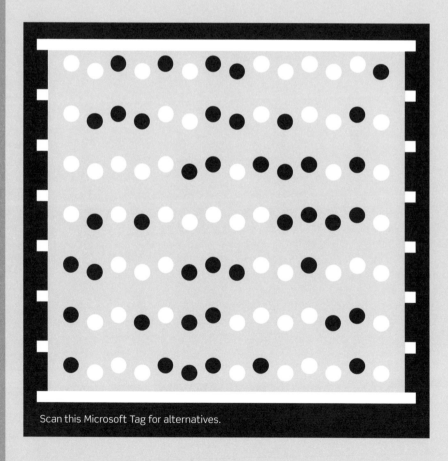

06
.TAG

Scan this Microsoft Tag for alternatives.

barcode from the supermarket.

All this together shapes the net: a virtually invisible web of lines across which data is exchanged between uniquely identified devices. While we get information from this net through the use of these devices, the net, meanwhile, keeps track of which device sends or receives what, where and when. The net gives and the net takes – and we live in the middle of it all.

Empowerment and Privacy Get a Spatial Dimension

Since the 1970s, social debate on information technology has been nourished by both *empowerment* as well as *privacy* discourse. In the *empowerment* discourse, the central question covers how information technology helps citizens organise and enrich their lives. IT, however, does not merely give; it takes.[14] The net registers what we do, when we do it, and with whom. This information can be useful for monitoring. This leads us to the other side of the net, the monitoring net. The limits of this surveillance are central in the *privacy* discourse: what kind of information may be collected about whom, and who may examine this data and for what purposes? The central question in *Check In / Check Out* is how these two discourses will change once we go *into* the net.

Empowerment: may and can you check in?

With the appearance of the World Wide Web and browsers in the 1990s, internet became accessible to the general public. Thanks to fast expansion of content, the net increasingly became a world of its own, where people could continue life separate from time and space. When you check in on the net, you enrich your virtual identity; you get more possibilities. When you check out, you cease to participate. This approach can be alluded to as the *empowerment* discourse, or the discussion on increasing potential through information technology.

In his trilogy *The Network Society*, Spanish sociologist Manuel Castells describes how internet helps people exchange information and money faster, within what he calls 'the space of flows' and 'timeless time'.[15] Where in the past people were dependent on each other's proximity for interaction and transaction, the internet offers an opportunity to distribute large amounts of data and money over large distances. With extensive casuistry he shows that especially large corporations manage the complexities of 'the space of flows' well, which helps them shed the restrictions of time and space. The stream of data and capital withdraws itself from government supervision, which consolidates the power of large corporations.

In part two of his trilogy, *The Power of Identity*[16], he shows how formerly suppressed groups, too, use the internet to liberate themselves from geographical limitations; in just a short time, they manage to get mobilised.[17] Philosopher Jos de Mul takes things a step further. Internet enables people to create new worlds. In *Cyberspace Odyssey*[18] he states that man's 'discovery' of cyberspace has created a new space for action: '*an ontological machine that produces possible worlds*'. In other words, information on the net is not only a derivative of reality outside the net; it also creates a new reality which has increasing influence over us. This gives new opportunities for action and causes us to constantly reconstruct our identities.

The first social question that is raised by this discourse is whether everybody can profit equally from these new opportunities. Is there no chance of a digital divide? Who are the vulnerable groups? Governments have set out to get citizens on-line. In the Netherlands we see that especially the programmes of the ministries of Finance and Education, Culture and Science are focused on empowerment. This does not only include net access, but also the right skills for using the net effectively. Europe, too, did its best for those who were in danger of lagging behind, namely small and medium sized companies, new EU countries and vulnerable groups in society, such as elderly and handicapped people. In Japan, policy makers noticed that not everyone was enjoying the Ubiquitous Network Society and consequently shifted their policy from U-Japan to i-Japan, where the 'I' stands for 'inclusive'.[19]

The emergence of the internet released us from space and time. With the digitalisation of public space, however, these two dimensions are returning. This raises the question of how the *empowerment* discourse will change with the shift from *on* the net to *in* the net. Van den Berg reflects on this question in her thesis *The Situated Self*.[20] Comparable to De Mul's analysis of cyberspace, she sees how people become overwhelmed by an increasing number of choices on how to shape their identities. Yet *Ambient Intelligence* magnifies this problem. In this case we no longer log in and out of cyberspace from our computers. We are increasingly surrounded by cyberspace; by computers that are becoming less and less visible. In more and more environments, our presence activates programmes that adjust the environment to our supposed wishes. Can we still stay clear of these programmes if we cannot see them? One person may make optimal use of this technology and easily switch between the many identities that have been granted to him, while another person may drown in his many selves. Not to mention the fearful vision of a smart environment that can impose identities on its users, thereby stigmatising them and take away their choices.

Privacy: may you and can you check out?

In the *privacy* discourse we can also see reflections on time and space. If you go on the net, you will leave traces which remain visible to others for a long time, across large distances. Here lurk the dangers of 'atmosphere crossings'.[21] Because digital media ignores limits of space and time,

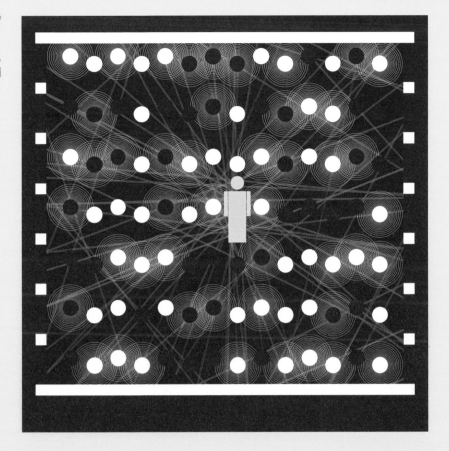

information collected on one person in one atmosphere, for example the atmospheres at work, at home, in medical or consumerist atmospheres, can easily cross into another atmosphere. This way, a person can become known in a different context from the one he wishes. For example, think of a spicy You Tube film that surfaces during a job interview, medical information that ends up in your circle of friends, or spending behaviour that turns out to be interesting to investigation services.

Privacy is an ambiguous concept. It can be defined as 'the worthiness of protection of personal space' or 'the right to be left alone'.[22] This right may seem self-evident, but it is not. In social traffic it is necessary to have a certain amount of information on each other in order to communicate and deal with each other. Total anonymity is practically impossible in our information society, but it is desirable to have some say over who knows what about you. Privacy is therefore not an absolute concept, but a relative one: it depends on the context and is subject to change over time.[23]

In the 1960s and 1970s, sensitivity to privacy in Europe and the US increased, not only with action groups and progressive citizens, but also politically. In the Netherlands, the 1971 census went hand in hand with many social protests, and the 1981 census was never even carried out.

Experiences from the Second World War played a large part; indeed, the registration of personal data had speeded up the persecution of the Jews. A call for the protection of privacy caused a discussion on the inclusion of privacy as a basic right.[24] This led to the addition of article 10 to the Dutch constitution:

1 Everyone shall have the right to respect for his privacy, without prejudice to restrictions laid down by or pursuant to Act of Parliament.
2 Rules to protect privacy shall be laid down by Act of Parliament in connection with the recording and dissemination of personal data.
3 Rules concerning the rights of persons to be informed of data recorded concerning them and of the use that is made thereof, and to have such data corrected shall be laid down by Act of Parliament.

This constitutional amendment led to the Data Protection Act in 1988. Debate flared up again when the European guidelines from 1995 had to be translated into national legislation. In 2001, the Data Protection Act was amended and became the new Dutch Data Protection Act. In this act it is established when something can be considered personal data and what requirements its processing has to adhere to. For instance, details such as name, address and date of birth may only be registered when this is 'necessary'; it must be clear who manages this data; this must be done in a just and discrete manner, and the person whose data has been collected must be offered an opportunity to have a look at this data and be able to change it. Since then, this act is being regulated by the Dutch Data Protection Authority.

Fair Information Principles

Every European nation has its own law on the protection of personal data, but they are all a national interpretation of the same European directive: the EC Directive 95/46/EC on the protection of individuals with regard to the processing of personal data and on the free movement of such data. The principles underlying this directive are, to a large extent, similar to the Privacy Guidelines adopted in 1980 by the OECD. In this study we focus on how people think personal data should be managed in daily life. We therefore extract the principles from the legislation in order to analyse how they would work in practice. Building on the work of Rotenberg (2003), Schermer (2007) summarises these principles as follows:

Collection Limitation Principle
Personal data should be obtained by lawful and fair means and, where appropriate, with the knowledge or consent of the data subject. Furthermore there should be limits to the collection of personal data.

Data Quality Principle
Personal data collected should be relevant to the purposes for which they are to be used and when used should be accurate, complete, and kept up-to-date.

Purpose Specification Principle
The purpose of the collection of any personal data should be specified no later than at the time of data collection and the subsequent use limited to the fulfilment of that purpose, or such others as are not incompatible with that purpose and as are specified on each occasion of change of purpose.

Use Limitation Principle

Personal data should not be disclosed, made available, or otherwise used for purposes other than those covered by the purpose specification.

Security Safeguards Principle

Personal data collected and used should be protected by reasonable security measures to minimise the risk of unauthorised access, destruction, use, modification or disclosure of personal data.

Openness Principle

There should be a general policy of openness about developments, practices and policies with respect to personal data. Means of establishing the existence and nature of personal data, the main purposes of their use, as well as the identity and residence of the data controller should be readily available.

Individual Participation Principle

A data subject should have the right to obtain confirmation from a data controller whether his information is being processed. Furthermore, the data subject has the right to have this information communicated to him within a reasonable time, in a reasonable manner, and in a form that is intelligible to him. If such information cannot be communicated, the data subject must be given reasons as to why it cannot be communicated, as well as the right to challenge this decision. Finally, the data subject has the right to challenge data relating to him, and if successful, have it erased, rectified, completed, or amended.

Accountability Principle

The final principle holds data controllers accountable for complying with measures that give effect to the above stated principles.

However, users of the net cannot always appeal to their privacy. The Dutch Data Protection Authority knows exceptions where safety is concerned. Therefore, investigation services fall under a different regime in the case of personal data use.

Since 2004, telecom providers are obliged by law to help investigation services to internet traffic information; in other words, who was where on the net, and when. This is the so-called data retention directive. On 7 July 2009, the Dutch Senate passed the Data Retention Act. Providers of public telecommunication networks and services are obliged by law to retain traffic and location data for a period of twelve months, in aid of locating and prosecuting serious crime.[25] Each time that you connect to the internet, telecom and internet providers must save, amongst other things, your name, address, town of residence, IP address, login name, telephone number, date and time of login and logout, and the internet services you used.[26] It concerns so-called *traffic and location data*, not the *contents* of the communication or the conversation. This is an implementation of the European guideline Data Retention, which states that data must be kept for a minimum of six and a maximum of 24 months.[27]

Lastly, there was the amendment in the Dutch Passport Act, where biometric characteristics in passports (digitalised facial scans and finger prints on the RFID chip) are saved in a central location and may be used for criminal investigation. On 11 June 2009, the Dutch Senate amended the Passport Act with respect to the reorganisation of the administration of travel documents. According to State Secretary Bijleveld, 'the choice for an on-line, central administration of travel documents is fundamentally inspired by the necessity to make the processes of applying for and issuing Dutch travelling documents more reliable'.[28] But as stated under article 4b, biometric data can also be used for 'investigating and prosecuting criminal offences' and 'conducting research into acts which pose a threat for the security of the state and other significant interests of one or more lands in the Kingdom or the security of allies'.[29] The expansion of the powers of criminal investigation met with little resistance (see case study Street Images).

The list of measures is far from complete, but we do believe the Netherlands has been more willing than other European countries to make personal data available for police investigation. Surprisingly enough, the introduction of all these measures go hand in hand with little political and social debate. The supervising net is embraced by citizens and politicians alike.

Privacy in public space

Is there attention for the influence of the digitalisation of public space on privacy? As not only more information becomes available about who does what, but also about where and when this person does this. An interesting point that arises here is that people usually log on to the net from their private spaces. Public space clearly is not private. What is the significance of the transition from being *on* the net to being *in* the net, in particular for the way that citizens experience their privacy? In other words, how can citizens protect their private lives in a public space?

In current European and Dutch policymaking circles we especially see discussions on the use of RFID: Radio Frequency IDentification. These small, remotely readable chips are used to identify smart cards and products. The chips can be used as a replacement for barcodes in order to trace goods in the logistics chain, and, once sold, to inform the consumer about the product. With smart cards, the chip can give each card a unique number and store information on the cardholder, such as personal data or credit. Each time the chip is read, for example upon granting access to something or upon completing a transaction, data on the user is stored. Perhaps what most led to privacy objections is that the chips can be read from a distance, possibly also by people who have no authority to do so. In this way, thieves could be able to tell if someone is carrying something valuable, and market researchers would see the kinds of products someone buys. However, because of the restricted reading-distance of the chips – a few centimetres to a few metres – chances of this happening are limited. Moreover, most RFID chips only emit a number, which only becomes meaningful in connection with the database of whoever supplied the chip. Nevertheless, monitoring people with microchips fuels the imagination and RFID has greatly boosted the privacy debate.

Euro officials Reding and Santucci have conducted various expert meetings and public consultations on RFID and privacy. In the Netherlands, especially the Ministry of Economic Afffairs is active on this file, assisted by the advice of the Data Protection Authority, the Consumers' Union, ECP-EPN and the Rathenau Institute. Here, too, the ambiguity between empowerment and privacy surfaces. RFID is seen as a promising technology, as long as privacy is safeguarded. The chips are convenient and help us monitor logistics chains and make them more efficient. However, as soon as the chip's number can lead back to a person, the Data Protection Act must apply. This called for some proposals for measures, such as the obligatory switching-off of chips in purchases or the application of labels to show customers that something contains an RFID chip. The use of RFID information by investigation services is taken for granted and only discussed within academic and activist circles.

A wide social discussion on the privacy aspects of the digitalisation of public space is therefore not yet taking place. Today, the use of CCTV and digital wicket gates is experienced as a natural part of society. That the scanning of mobile traffic data not only traces who calls whom, but also where and when, likewise caused little turmoil in the Netherlands.

Identity Management: Giving and Taking Control

The requisites for empowerment and privacy in digital public space seem conflicting, to a certain extent. From an empowerment standpoint, the use of data systems is encouraged, because it will make people better off. From a privacy standpoint, this use is actually discouraged.

If you would like to use data systems, you must somehow identify yourself. If you completely cling on to privacy, you will not be known; you will have no access and receive no information. However, matters are actually subtler than this. It is not only about whether you are known by data systems. It is also about your identity and how it is managed. *How* are you known and by *whom*? We therefore introduce the concept *Identity Management* (IdM), which contains empowerment as well as safeguarded privacy.

The concept Identity Management is used both in social academic literature and in technical literature, although in very different ways. Sociologists and psychologists already used this concept in the 1980s and 1990s in order to analyse how people try to influence how they are seen by others. This implies for example one's ethnicity[30], age[31], or sexual preferences.[32] These sociologists do not see human identity as a given; rather as something that constantly gets construed socially through interaction with others. Meanwhile, the term is being used in management literature in order to describe how businesses can best design their databases, and what kinds of business advantages this provides. Identity Management here concerns the safe management of access to systems, in other words identification (someone logs in), authentication (he is whom he claims to be) and authorisation (he may perform actions within the system).[33] Numerically, technical studies publicise most on IdM. Many definitions of IdM are of a technical nature, such as the following: 'processes and all underlying technologies for the creation, management and use of identity data'.[34]

In recent years, technical and social disciplines seem to somewhat meet each other. This is because sociologists and psychologists have started researching how people manage their digital identity on-line, for example through the use of a pseudonym, avatars in virtual worlds, and photos and stories on social websites.[35] Technical experts have paid more attention to social subjects such as trust, user-friendliness and privacy.[36]

08
.TAG

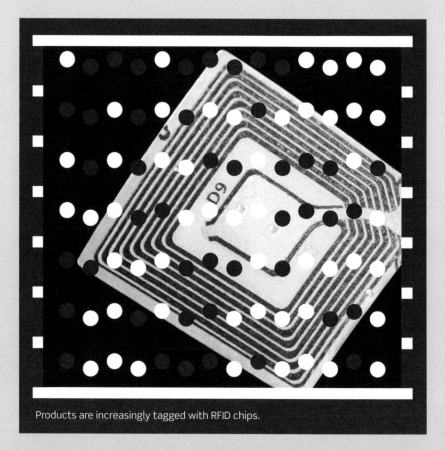

Products are increasingly tagged with RFID chips.

The goal of the European PRIME project (Privacy and Identity Management for Europe) is: 'individual's sovereignty over their personal data', and 'to enable individuals to negotiate with service providers the disclosure of personal data and conditions defined by their preferences and privacy policy'.[37] In this interpretation of Identity Management, elements of empowerment (autonomy over personal data) meet elements of privacy.

However, the sociological side largely lacks in definitions. We are speaking of the social image that other data system users get on a given person based on the data in that system. That constructed social image consequently leads to a judgement: has that person paid, does he get access, and so on. Through the use of data systems, people get an increasingly richer virtual identity next to their physical identity – in other words, an identity that is visible to other users within the system, irrespective of time and space. This identity does not necessarily need to be linked to the name of this person. It can be a number with which someone logs in, which, although it may not be a formal piece of personal data, will still have consequences for that person: price differentiation, denied access and so on.

A rich identity offers users empowerment: he may get access to information and services in the system, because his identity helps others in judging him. However, if this identity does not correspond to how the physical person behind it wishes to be known, or if the wrong person has access to this identity, he may be judged in an undesirable way and his privacy is at issue. If you log into a shopping website, for example, you would like to be known as the customer who, in the past, has always paid his bills on time and values certain offers. However, if your identity leads to the seller's suspicion, or to unwanted advertising, something went wrong. The importance of good Identity Management does not only mean that someone is known, but especially how and by whom. A social constructivist vision on Identity Management, therefore, emphasises that people must get grip on the way in which they provide each other access to information that leads to mutual judgement. There must be a good balance between giving and taking control – privacy and empowerment.

Identity Management in this Book

Check In / Check Out researches in what way Identity Management takes place in our digitalised public space. We will do this referring to five cases – contactless smart cards in public transport, 'networked' driving (think GPS and pay-as-you-drive), Near Field Communication, CCTV, Google Earth and Street View – and a chapter in which we sketch the future scenario of a

Living Map. Within the framework of these cases, we compare and contrast the Dutch situation with international examples, especially from Europe and Japan.

In the first case study, *Gated Stations*, we describe a network of wicket gates within which contactless smart cards make your travelling behaviour transparent and checkable. Identity Management is then about deciding who may link the number on the card to your name and who may look into your travelling data. While many big Asian cities implemented these systems just to speed up the flow of travellers and let it run next to other systems, the Dutch are aiming towards a single, national control system. In doing so, they are confronted with an ever growing resistance. In an attempt at resolving the controversy we encounter many kinds of Identity Management issues.

In *Networked Cars,* we discuss the many parties that use systems to see where your car is, to charge you for the distances you travelled, to show you the way, and to avoid traffic jams. Proposals by the Dutch government for dynamic roadpricing systems during the last 20 years have failed, while the Dutch company TomTom is world leader in car navigation devices. It appears that the government division on traffic management is becoming increasingly dependent on businesses like these, and many objectives for tracking cars are confusing. You no longer know who knows what about you and your car, and at the same time, options are limited for you to manage your identity yourself.

In *Money Mobiles,* we describe a network of mobile phones that read out their environments. Paying with your mobile, opening doors, and retrieving information from a film poster: it's all possible with Near Field Communication. NFC is an interesting case indeed, because with this, information is linked to your location through various technologies: GSM, GPRS, internet and RFID. Providers do this in order to gain more insight into and control over your purchasing behaviour. However, if so many technologies and organisations are being linked to each other, it becomes unclear who manages your identity. Although more than half the Japanese phones have this application, it is still rather unknown in the rest of the world. We therefore contrast the Japanese system with international developments and some pilot projects in the Netherlands.

In the case study *Street Images*, we take a look behind the scenes of CCTV. We see how a network of images is created. Whether streets, stations and tunnels are becoming safer because of the cameras is hard to verify; nevertheless, the demand for surveillance is big. We see that the number of cameras is increasing, they are becoming more intelligent, images are being exchanged within larger and larger networks and citizens, too, more often provide images. As a passerby you create an identity in these systems, but the person who watches you within the system must also be identified. This chapter shows how the regulating watchful eyes are regulated themselves.

In *Geoweb*, we describe how the surface of the Earth has been digitally captured by satellite imagery and aerial photographs and made publicly

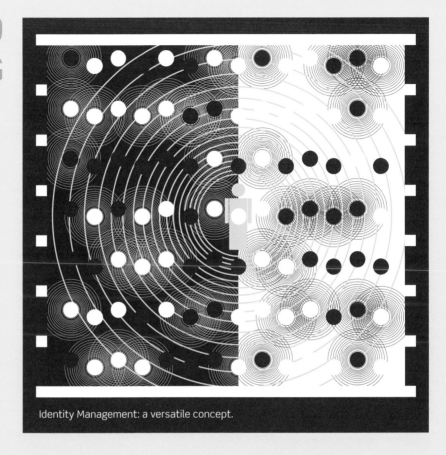

Identity Management: a versatile concept.

available through services like Google Earth. With Street View you can have a digital stroll along any random street. You can use this information to find the way; to gain information on the world around you. But how much of yourself are you ready to relinquish? We describe the roles that Google Earth and Street View play on the net; we will also cover services that provide live information on digital public space.

The Living Map is a case on a possible future. Imagine that all data from digital public space could be placed live on a map. Who would be allowed to see this? What would you like to see yourself? Design sessions with citizens, experts and governmental officials resulted in many possible applications. Still, more important is how they evaluated the digitalisation of public space and what it means for them to have entered this new phase in the information society.

In the closing chapter we draw our conclusions from the case studies and sketch *Identity Management in the net*. What kinds of trends can you expect? How should your identity be managed in digital public space? We will provide a series of design principles that will help shape this new phase in information society, so not only businesses and authorities, but also you as a citizen, will receive optimal benefits.

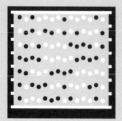

TAG for note 6

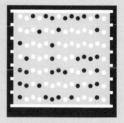

TAG for note 8

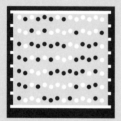

TAG for note 9

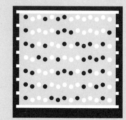

TAG for note 10

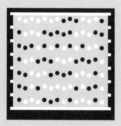

TAG for note 11

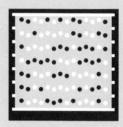

TAG for note 27

Notes

1 Kok, M. de (1983). De informatiemaatschappij: De gevolgen van de micro-elektronische revolutie. Maastricht: Natuur en Techniek.

2 Rathenau, G.W. (1980). Maatschappelijke gevolgen van de micro-elektronica: Rapport van de adviesgroep Rathenau. The Hague: Ministry of Education, Culture and Science.

3 Veraart, F. (2008). Vormgevers van persoonlijk computergebruik: De ontwikkeling van computers voor kleingebruikers in Nederland, 1970-1990. Eindhoven: Stichting Historie der Techniek.

4 Haan, J. de, C. van 't Hof & R. van Est (2006). 'De digitale generatie'. In: Haan J. de & C. van 't Hof (red.) (2006). Jaarboek ICT en samenleving: De digitale generatie. Amsterdam: Boom.

5 Idem Haan, J. de, C. van 't Hof & R. van Est (2006).

6 Schilpzand, W. & C. van 't Hof (2008). RFID as the Key to the Ubiquitous Network Society. A Japanese Case Study on Identity Management. The Hague: Rathenau Institute in collaboration with TU Eindhoven and the Dutch Embassy in Japan.

7 Weiser, M. (1991). 'The Computer for the 21st Century'. In: Scientific American, September 1991.

8 Greenfield, A. (2006). Everyware: The Dawning Age of Ubiquitous Computing. Berkely: New Riders.

9 Berg, B. van den (2009). The Situated Self. Identity in a World of Ambient Intelligence. (dissertation) Rotterdam: Erasmus Universiteit.

10 Srivastava, L. (2005). The Internet of Things. Geneva: ITU Internet Reports.

11 Interview Christian van 't Hof (20 August 2010) with Songlin Feng, president of the Shanghai Advanced Research Institute.

12 Source: http://www.microsoft.com/tag For downloading free scanning software: http://gettag.mobi/

13 You can create the codes for free at: http://qrcode.kaywa.com/

14 Beek, K. van, et al. (2001). Controle geven of nemen: Een politieke agenda voor de informatiesamenleving. Amsterdam: Infodrome.

15 Castells, M. (1996). The Rise of the Network Society. Vol. 1 of The Information Age: Economy, Society and Culture. Oxford-UK: Blackwell Publishers.

16 Castells, M. (1997). The Power of Identity. Vol. 2 of The Information Age: Economy, Society and Culture. Oxford-UK: Blackwell Publishers.

17 In his later work, The Internet Galaxy (2004), he pays attention to what he calls: 'The geography of the internet'. Current centres of power, especially in large Western cities, appear to have better networks than other cities. In short, even though data can be exchanged from everywhere and at all times, power will remain where it is.

18 Mul, J. de (2002). Cyberspace Odyssee. Kampen: Uitgeverij Klement.

19 Interview Christian van 't Hof (3 July 2009) with Ishima en Sanao Orri, Ministry of Internal Affairs and Communication, Tokyo.

20 Idem Berg, B. van den (2009).

21 Schermer, B.W. (2008). Ambient Intelligence, persoonsgegevens en consumentenbescherming. The Hague: ECP-EPN.

22 Vuijsje, H. (1998). 'De burger en de datakloon. Over persoonsgegevens en solidariteit'. In: Privacy geregistreerd. Visions on the social meaning of privacy. The Hague: Rathenau Institute.

23 Gutwirth, S. (2002). Privacy and the Information Age. Oxford: Rowman & Littlefield Publishers.

24 Idem Vuijsje, H. (1998).

25 Dutch Senate, introduced bill: Data Retention Act. Source: http://www.eerstekamer.nl/wetsvoorstel/31145_wet_bewaarplicht

26 XS4ALL. 'Wat er bewaard moet worden onder de bewaarplicht'. Source: http://www.xs4all.nl/opinie/wat-er-bewaard-moet-worden-onder-de-bewaarplicht/

27 Guideline no. 06/24/EG from the European Parliament and the Council (guideline data retention), 15 March 2006.

28 Amendment of the Dutch Passport Act in connection with the reorganisation of travel document administration. Statement of answer, parliamentary paper 130536, 28 April 2009.

29 Kingdom Act for the amendment of the Dutch Passport Act in connection with the reorganisation of travel document administration, 11 June 2009.

30 Mummendey, A. et al. (1999). 'Socio-structural characteristics of intergroup relations and Identity Management strategies: results from a field study in East Germany'. In: European Journal of Social Psychology, vol. 29, no. 2-3, pp. 259-285.

31 Biggs, S. (1997). 'Choosing Not To Be Old? Masks, Bodies and Identity Management in Later Life'. In: Ageing & Society, 17, pp. 553-570.

32 Blanz, M. et al. (1998). 'Responding to negative social identity: a taxonomy of Identity Management strategies'. In: European Journal of Social Psychology, vol. 28, no. 5, pp. 697-729.

33 Marbus, R. (2009). Identity Management in Nederland. Stand van zaken. The Hague: ECP-EPN.

34 Ducaste, N. et al. (2008). Exploring Identity Management and Trust. The Hague: Expertise Centrum, p. 214.

35 Suler, J. (2002). 'Identity Management in Cyberspace'. In: Journal of Applied Psychoanalytic Studies, vol. 4, no. 4.

36 Idem Marbus, R. (2009).

37 Source: https://www.prime-project.eu

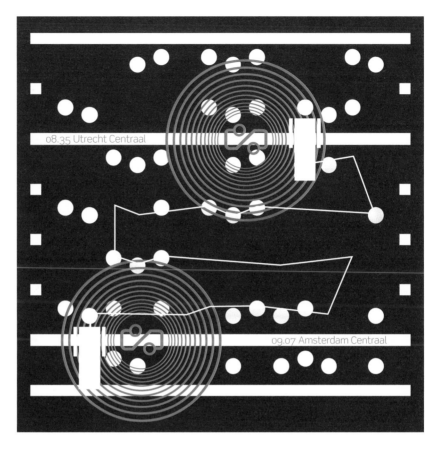

08.35 Utrecht Centraal

09.07 Amsterdam Centraal

Case 0001

Gated Stations

Christian van 't Hof

'...one closed off national

control system, where

all travellers will be linked

to a 16-digit number...'

Smart Cards as the Key to a Digitalised Public Transport

During the last decade, many big cities throughout the world shifted from tickets to smart card based systems in public transport. Travellers do not only pay with their cards, they check in and out of a network with a unique number. While most of these systems are only used for transactions, the travel data are sometimes used for other purposes too, which, in some cases, led to public controversies. The case of the Netherlands is unique in that regard. The Dutch aim for one national system for all public transport and to use it as a control system too. Also, the Netherlands has a tradition of open public debate among many stakeholders before reaching a decision – the so-called polder culture – which brings all controversial issues out in the open.

This case study shows how digitalised public transport can provide public transport companies with valuable information on their customers and means of control. It also shows the importance of civil counterforces in giving the users of a system a voice. Still, as the means to empower the users of the system were mainly neglected, Identity Management boils down to privacy issues concerning personal data, and who should be allowed to use this data and for which purpose. Still, the aims of the transport companies will only be fulfilled when all travellers in public transport use only this one system. It remains to be seen whether this will ever happen.

0001 .0001 The Digitalisation of Public Transport

In the digitalised public transport you don't just buy a ticket, you check in and out with a RFID smart card. Other than paper tickets, coins or magnetic cards, these systems allow transport companies to track the locations where travellers get in and out of public transport vehicles or stations. This solves at least one problem: if travellers buy their tickets at one company, but travel with another, the system can calculate who needs to pay whom. Moreover, these systems promise to speed up the flow of travellers, as transactions are made by just swiping a card on a reader. It is therefore at the most congested transport hubs where we can see these systems being applied first: Hong Kong, Tokyo, London and the Netherlands. Although these systems all work on similar technologies, we observe many cultural differences in their implementation.

0001 .0001 .0001 Efficiency in transactions

Hong Kong was the first. Their Octopus system was launched in 1997 and promised to speed up transactions and bring an end to the problem of coin shortage. Due to its success, it has been an example for the rest of the world ever since. The card contains a FeliCa RFID chip from Sony. It can be an anonymous prepaid card or a personal one linked to a credit card. Travellers can also opt for a discount card that only registers whether they are under or above a certain age, without containing any other personal information. Another trait is its interoperability: personalised cards can also be used as access key to enter buildings. Students use it to record their attendance and library loans. The latest figure on its use was 20 million in 2009.[1]

The biggest in the world are currently the London Oystercard and the Japanese SUICA: both with about 30 million users.[2] The SUICA, or Super Urban Intelligent CArd, also contains the FeliCa chip and was launched in 2001 by JR East. It can be used at all hundred and one public transport providers in the Tokyo metropolitan area (train, subways and buses). The main objectives of these public transport providers were efficiency and convenience: speeding up the flow of travellers and providing them a new means of payment for other purchases too, such as food and services around the stations. A particular feature here is the Mobile FeliCa, or a chip that is integrated into a mobile phone. (See case study *Money Mobiles*)

RFID as key to the digitalised public transport network

Countries may differ in the way they implement electronic payment systems in public transport, but the technology behind it is quite similar. What you see as a traveller is your smart card and a range of reading devices placed at the bus drivers, the turnstiles of the subway or entrances train stations. What you don't see is how a small chip inside your card exchanges numbers with a complex network behind the readers. This is how it works.

The key technology is RFID, which stands for Radio Frequency Identification. The card contains a RFID chip, which is a small processor wrapped up in an antenna that serves as a coil. If the card is in the proximity of a few centimetres of a reader, it catches its signal (13.54 MHz) and uses it to generate energy for sending back a signal. When both devices recognise each other, data is exchanged: the ID of the card and reader, time, transaction, etc. The location is determined by the station it is at, or the GPS coordinates of the vehicle. Some readers, like those in London busses, work with fixed tariffs, and deduct a certain amount of money from your smart card once you check in. Most readers first deduct a higher price from the card and give a partial restitution when checking out. Readers also contain black lists of cards that might be stolen or tempered with.

The network behind the readers consists of different layers. The reader first stores the data exchange on its local database, from which it is transferred periodically to the database of the transport company and finally to a central database. This so called buffering of data is essential for making the system fast and robust. Transactions are quicker, because the data is only exchanged locally. In case of a network disruption, data is not lost as it is always stored in one of the databases in-between. The system cannot provide a live image of all transactions, as there is always a time lag of one or two days between the transaction and the centralised exchange, in case of the Dutch public transport smart card – the so-called OV-chip card.

In the Netherlands there are three kinds of OV-chip cards: a disposable ticket, an anonymous card and a personal card. The cards contain a MiFare Classic chip of 4 kB, which is divided into 40 sectors, each with its own encryption key. It contains information on the value stored, where the card is purchased and the last ten trips (location, time, vehicle and price). Personal cards also store a date of birth. Name and photo are only printed on the card, not stored.

The ID of the card consists of a unique number of 16 digits. This is your ID, which is managed by the transport companies. If you use an anonymous card, you are just a number along with your transactions. In the case of a personalised card, the 16 digit number can be linked to your name, address, date of birth, social security number, photograph and the like. Who is allowed to connect these IDs and under what circumstances has been a matter of continuous debate.

0001 .0001 .0010 One system for everything

The prime motivation for Dutch public transport companies to go electronic was to get rid of the paper ticket. In the Netherlands, a paper ticket was and still is used, on which a set of zones could be stamped off; the so-called 'zone card' or, in Dutch, the 'strippenkaart'. Travellers can buy this card at one public transport company and use it at another. As a result, the travel companies needed to come up with a very complicated key to annually balance incomes and costs amongst each other. The electronic

11
.TAG

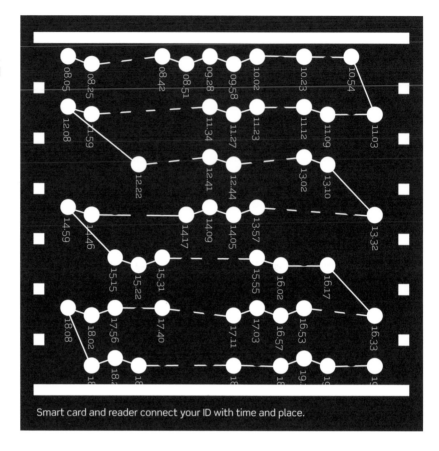

Smart card and reader connect your ID with time and place.

system does this automatically, on a daily basis. Travellers find the electronic system easier too, as they do not have to calculate their travel zones before hand; rather, they just check in and out and have the calculation made for them.

Plans for using a smart card within the Dutch public transport system started in 1999. This smart card is called the OV-chip card, where OV stands for public transport, or, in Dutch, 'openbaar vervoer'. The initiative was led by three municipal transport companies (RET in Rotterdam, GVB in Amsterdam and HTM in The Hague) and Connexxion, a regional bus company. When the Dutch Railways, the NS, also joined, the plan evolved to one system for all public transport in the Netherlands. To execute all transactions, they formed the consortium Trans Link Systems.

With one national digital system, besides the fair exchange of incomes and costs, other functions and ambitions[3] could be added. First, the system would allow for more price differentiation, for example, an increase in prices during rush hour and a decrease in prices during off-peak hours. Secondly, data on travellers opens up opportunities for direct marketing. If people visit a station often, local businesses can give them offers to attract them. Travellers could also be advised to buy season tickets.

Third, the card could also be used by travellers as a more universal payment system, e.g. for buying a sandwich at the train station.

Once the system is fully closed off and only accessible by OV-chip card, the database of transactions can provide a full image of the number of people who use which vehicles, and when. A fourth aim is then to use this as management information, for example to analyse which lines are used more often than others and how the fleet of vehicles can be adjusted accordingly. Users might be given access to this information too, so they can choose to adapt their travelling behaviour according to the crowdedness on the lines.

Finally, and most important for at least the NS (Dutch Railways) and the RET (Rotterdam), the OV-chip system would solve many security issues. Fare dodging is a common problem in the Dutch trains and subways. The companies not only lose money on people who do not pay; many fare dodgers show much aggression once they are discovered and forced to pay the fine. Also, stations in the Netherlands tend to attract many homeless people, drug addicts and vandals. Gated stations, accessible only after a valid electronic transaction, would then be a place for paying and well-behaving travellers only.

These ambitions can only be achieved once the system is totally closed off with gates where travellers check in and out. The city of Rotterdam was the first to have fully closed off public transport, on 29 January 2009. This satisfied RET, since running two systems side by side was costing 200.000 Euros a month. Amsterdam followed on 27 August 2009. Both are now able to beat fare dodging and count all identities checking in and out of their systems. It is still an ambition to make the whole Dutch public transport system closed off.[4] But other than in the big Asian cities, where just one company lays a new system next to the old one, implementing a single Dutch national system depends on the cooperation of a complex constellation of many parties, and it is bound to lead to public controversy.

0001 .0001 .0011 Public controversy

Dutch political culture is characterised by open and lively public debate. Moreover, it is normal to involve various stakeholders in developing public policies. As a result, civil organisations, which in principle have little formal power over a certain policy making process, can have an important voice in the media and the political debate. The development and implementation of the Dutch OV-chip card illustrates this Dutch political culture, since it is surrounded by the involvement of many societal organisations and public controversy.

Dutch public transport companies are linked to local, regional and national governments through licences, infrastructure and grants. For example, NS received 500 million euro from the Dutch Ministry of Public Transport and Waterworks in 2001 for the implementation of the card. This ministry also sets the rates for travel prices through the Persons Travel Act, as do the municipalities for the local companies. This constellation of many organisations combined with the ambitious targets make the OV-chip card system a very complex project.

The first trials started in 2004 with Connexxion busses in southern regions, and in 2005 also on all public transport in and around Rotterdam. Amsterdam followed in 2006. By then, a constellation of many civil organisations[5] form the National Consumers Council (Landelijk Consumenten Overleg). They file a pamphlet, stating their demands. The OV-chip card should make travelling easier and not more expensive. Price differentiation and calculation should be transparent. Public transport should remain evenly accessible for vulnerable groups such the elder and handicapped. Sufficient service levels should remain and the system must be reliable for travellers (no malfunctioning). They also state that traveller privacy must be guaranteed. After some deliberation, the council concluded in January 2007 that none of the demands were met. Ever since, they promote the idea of a dual system: let the old system run next to the new one and let travellers decide which one to use.

Meanwhile, another party joined their ranks: the Dutch Data Protection Agency (DPA). In its statement 'Privacy and the OV-chip card' from 10 November 2005, the agency urged transport companies to comply with the guidelines of the Data Protection Act. Their message was taken up by the media and parliament, urging the minister to take appropriate action. The transport companies responded with a code of conduct for the handling of personal data, which was filed at court on 21 June 2007. The DPA continued its investigations and discovered that the GVB in Amsterdam was using too much personal data in inappropriate ways and filed a complaint at the Ministry of Transport. The GVB was forced to lower their marketing efforts and take better care of securing personal data. From then on, the DPA is allowed to audit every transportation company every two years.

As the new system was used more frequently and in more places, another problem came to light: many travellers who check in at the bus, tram or train, forget to check out again. This leads to higher prices, as the system first deducts the highest possible fare (4 Euros on trams, buses and subways, 20 Euros on trains) at checking in and calculates the real price at checking out. If travellers discover they paid too much, it is difficult for them to get their money back. Numerous accounts are reported in the media. The exact amount of so-called 'unfulfilled transactions' is difficult to calculate, but sums up to quite some money. For example, the municipality of Rotterdam claimed that only 0.44 per cent of all transactions were unfulfilled.[6] According to research by the Green Party, it amounts to 2.5 per cent in Amsterdam, or 6.6 million travellers, amounting to 12.5 million Euros annually.[7]

Subscription card holders also faced problems, as they generally don't check in and out. They feel they have already paid and see no point in performing the transaction. To the transport companies however, their 16-digit number escapes their monitor, leaving them with incomplete management information. They therefore decided to fine these travellers 35 Euros for fare dodging. Besides the fact that this is perceived as unfair, it is also a question whether this is legal.[8]

Other problems arose when the transport companies started to close off the stations and make them gated. Some claimed the gates were hostile to people with disabilities. Others claim they may trap crowds in case of an emergency. Moreover, closing off a station is also perceived as privatising public space. In the city of Leiden for example, the station is a gateway between two sides of the city, which can only be bypassed through some faraway, dark tunnels. Protest Groups therefore held actions at the station on 14 March 2007. Local politicians joined in and stated towards the media, 'away with the gates'.[9]

Finally, computer scientist succeeded in hacking the system at several occasions between May 2007 and March 2008, proving important leaks in its security. The Dutch parliament then decided to put the implementation of the card on a temporary hold. Huizinga, then Secretary of State and responsible for the project, almost lost her post in the controversy and came up with a 'plan of attack to beat the negative image of the OV-chip card' on 29 February 2009. She addressed the issues of the card's security, its pricing, privacy and, most importantly, who will lead the project. Making stations gated remained on the agenda, but she refrained from mentioning a date. Then the Dutch government fell. Yet again, transport companies were on their own against an ever-growing civil resistance.

0001 Managing Identities in
.0010 Digitalised Public Transport

The Dutch case of digitalised public transport teaches us how the identities of travellers can be used for many purposes, and what exactly is at stake. Privacy issues revolve around the use of travel data for marketing and police investigation, while identities can also be forged by computer experts. The Dutch seem to accept the concept of digitalised public transport as a means of control. In practice, Identity Management therefore boiled down to privacy issues, with few opportunities for user empowerment.

0001 Opting in or out for direct marketing
.0010
.0001
Direct marketing is a form of advertising products or services to a specific individual instead of broadcasting it. In the digitalisation of public space, businesses get increasingly specific insights into the behaviour of people, which provides them opportunities for targeting them more specifically. To prevent citizens from being hassled all the time, the Data Protection Act applies. This Act states that personal data should only be used if strictly necessary, and if the person in question is informed about it.

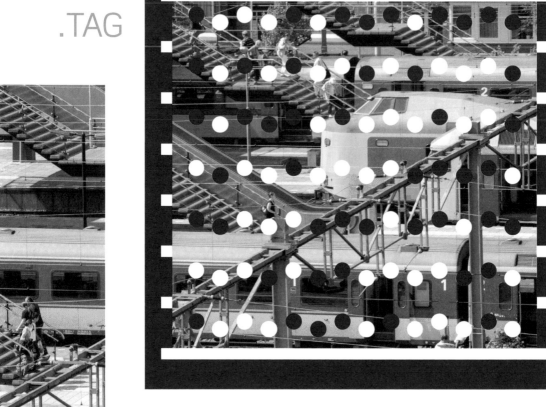

Still, what is really 'necessary', when is someone really 'informed' and when is data 'personal'?

In case of the OV-chip card, transport companies first aimed to use the travel data as input for their direct marketing efforts. For example, if you cross one station often, you'll receive a coupon for a sandwich discount via e-mail. To comply with the demands of the Data Protection Agency, the transport companies state in their 2007 Guideline that they will use travel data for direct marketing unless the customer asks them not to. This form of informed consent is known as an 'opt-out' regime. The Data Protection Agency did not agree with this, claiming this way of marketing is not really necessary for their businesses and it does not provide a clear choice for the customers.[10]

After years of public debate and the mediation of the Secretary of State, the DPA and the transport companies came to the following agreement. Naturally, name, address, gender and age are perceived as personal data. In case of the OV-chip card, travelling data as well as the 16-digit number are considered to be personal. Travellers can now read on the OV-chip card website what is actually happening with their personal data.[11] Only the consortium Trans Link Systems has a total overview of all data, but they are not allowed to do any marketing. If you bought a personalised card at one of the transport companies, they have to delete your personal data after sending it to Trans Link Systems. Only if you purchased a travel product (e.g. a season ticket) can this company monitor your travel behaviour and send you marketing. If marketing involves advice about travelling, this is seen as necessary for the company's business and an opt-out regime applies. For all other marketing efforts, the transport companies need to adhere to an opt-in regime.

This controversy is in sheer contrast with the Japanese situation. Japan recently gained a Data Protection Directive too, but it is merely enforced. Being a 'shaming culture' instead of a 'blaming culture', companies go great lengths to stay in their customers' favour. In 2003 and 2004, a number of articles appeared in Japanese transport magazines about the possibilities for personalised marketing with the SUICA. In these articles, the authors speculated on the possibilities of personalised offers on the basis of a client's travelling history. When we confronted JR East with these ideas, they told us expressly that they were not planning on using the SUICA-databases for marketing purposes anytime soon. JR East fears a scandal if users feel that JR East is misusing their data, whether justified or not.[12]

0001 .0010 .0010 Hacking the card

Information security is a continuous battle between those who apply cryptography to prevent unwanted intrusion on information systems and those who take enough effort to crack the code. Any information system can be hacked, as long as you take enough time to find the key. At the start of the OV-chip card project, the cryptography of its chip was seen as sufficiently secure. But as the system became more widely used and more notorious, so did its appeal as a hacker's trophy.[13] The first successful hacks were the single use cards, which have a lighter security level. Next were the chips on anonymous and personalised cards, the MiFare Classic from NXP. On 7 March 2008, the Digital Security Group at the Radboud University Nijmegen succeeded in solving the cryptological puzzle and got access to the card. They were able to read the cards, find out the users' travelling behaviour and manipulate its deposit value.[14]

Hacking the MiFare Classic wasn't about getting free rides on buses, it was about showing serious flaws in the security of a chip of which NXP already sold about a billion and which was also used in access keys for governmental buildings. Professor Bart Jacobs, leader of the DSG, therefore took a more careful approach. He first warned the Dutch security authorities, the minister of Internal Affairs, NXP and Trans Link Systems about their achievement, so they could take proper action.[15] Dutch parliament decided to put the implementation of the card on a temporary hold.

NXP went to court in order to prevent researchers from publishing their results, and lost. Trans Link Systems (TLS) opened a scientific forum for securing the card and ordered the Dutch research organisation TNO to analyse the risks of the hacked card. TNO claims that the risk is acceptable, as the effort to break the code and issue new cards outweigh the perceived benefits of fare dodging. A round table meeting in parliament therefore concluded: it's just not a criminal business case.[16]

Jacobs, head of research, finds this most extraordinary, and states that 'the OV-chip card is like an open wallet'. Researchers Teepe and Hoepman argue that 'if you hack a system once, it is much easier to do it a second time'. Moreover, these researchers condemn the defensive attitude of TLS and NXP. If they would have collaborated with the computer science community, all this would not have happened.[17]

The Digital Security Group therefore started building their own card: OV-chip card 2.0.[18]

Travel data for police investigation

0001
.0010
.0011

Travel data are of interest for police investigation and, as described in the first chapter, legislation is continuously being adapted for this purpose. Can police use data on people checking in and out of digitalised public transport? As a matter of fact, they do. Still, it is debated under what circumstances they are allowed to and for what purposes.

The first reports on the London Oyster Card in 2006 were made by *The Observer*. According to this British newspaper, the London police are very interested in using the journey data that are stored about travellers who use the Oyster card. Already in January 2004, a total of 61 requests were filed in that month alone. In a response, a spokesperson from Transport for London stated that 'a very few authorised individuals can access this data and there is...no bulk disclosure of personal data to any law enforcement agency. If information is disclosed, it is always done so in accordance with the Data Protection Act after a case-by-case evaluation.'[19] This response reveals a very fundamental point: security services can demand the Oyster records of specific individuals under investigation to establish where they have been, but they cannot trawl the whole database to see whether someone might show a particular profile. During our visit in Japan, we also enquired whether the Tokyo police would use travel data. While no official data are available, both JR East and the police department acknowledge that it happens.[20]

With this knowledge, we went to the Dutch public and politicians. On 4 April 2007, Rathenau organised a public debate together with ECP on RFID and privacy. The question was raised whether data can be used for police investigation. Members of the Socialist Party and the Labour Party claim this was not the purpose of the card. Right wing politicians from the Christian Democrats and the Liberal Party, however, claim that police should make use of all data available. Crime fighter Fred Teeven from the Liberal Party even proposed a fully personalised system, 'to keep criminals out of public transport'. This statement was used in an opinion poll later on.

Outside the scope of the media, a first incident took place. On 6 May 2007, a woman was harassed at one of the metro stations in Rotterdam. The prosecutor therefore claimed all the travel data from that station on that night. They were allowed to do so, due to the Dutch laws on police enquiry. In the court case that followed, TLS claimed the prosecutor was not permitted to also see all the photographs of the card holders, as this is defined as 'sensitive' data from which ethnicity or religion can be deduced. Therefore, the photos had to be returned, but the police did get all the other data.[21]

0001 .0010 .0100 Public responses

The success of electronic payment systems in public transport is generally stated in terms of the numbers of travellers willing to switch. SUICA and Octopus show rapid growth rates that demonstrate the acceptance of the cards. This does not work for the Netherlands, as the transport companies aim for a single system only, with no option other than to use the OV-chip card. Another source for measuring acceptance is to analyse the complaints that these systems receive. Finally, surveys were held which reveal that travellers do accept the principle of gated stations, but are critical towards the way the OV-chip card is implemented.

The Japanese SUICA can be seen as a success in terms of the acceptance of travellers. Not only did sales figures exceed the expectations of JR East; the number of complaints is nearly negligible. A visit to the National Consumer Affairs Centre revealed that of 1.1 million complaints that they received in 2006, only 93 were related to IC cards in general, among which SUICA. That equals to less than 0.01 per cent of total complaints. In a system with more than 10 million daily uses, that's fairly slim. An essential aspect of the SUICA system that helped its adoption was the presence of railway staff at the ticket gates.[22]

The Netherlands show a very different picture. User rates grow too slowly, leading to all sorts of discount offers to attract people to use the cards, while people with a subscription even receive an OV-chip card unasked for. Rotterdam had to execute tremendous force to get all travellers to use the card, as they wanted to close off stations on 29 January 2009. At the beginning of the month, only 30 per cent were using it, while the last 40 per cent of them only switched on the last day.[23] Since then, there has been no alternative way of paying. A count of complaints also shows a different picture. The national office of the OV-chip card itself receives about 700 a month, while the OV-chip complaint site of the Dutch Green party gets about a 1000 per month.[24]

Public surveys, however, show a more nuanced image. Research by the Rathenau Institute[25] shows that people generally see the advantage of the system, but they are slightly disappointed in its daily practice. In our survey, 64 per cent considered the card positive, while 11 per cent were negative about it. The main objection is that people tend to forget to check out and end up paying the full price. Also, many mention the malfunctioning of readers. Some mention the aspect of losing their privacy, but this element is seen as negative when it comes to marketing, while positive when it comes to security.

We therefore posed questions on whether the OV-chip card should be used for police investigation. When it comes to tracking suspects, 72 per cent agree, while 18 per cent disagree. For tracking witnesses, 62 per cent are in favour and 24 per cent are against it. A majority of 58 per cent agreed with and 16 per cent were against a statement about aiming for a totally personalised public transport 'in order to keep criminals out of public transport'.[26] This indicates that the Dutch seem to accept the concept of digitalised public transport as a control system.

0001 .0011 Conclusions

Cities throughout the world are shifting from public transport tickets to digitalised systems where travellers check in and out. Although the technologies used are quite similar, cultures show many differences in the implementation of it. In big Asian cities, travellers have the option to be either anonymous, linked to a number or identified. They deliberately adhere to the principle that the new system has to prove itself before the old one is discarded. Digitalisation is about efficiency and convenience. In this the Netherlands is unique, on the other hand, as it aims towards one closed off national control system, where all travellers will be linked to a 16-digit number, locked to the time and places they check in and out. Here, Identity Management in digitalised public transport is about what the unique number on the card says about you as a traveller, and who is allowed to access this information, under what conditions.

Privacy issues mainly resolve around hacking, marketing and police investigation. Dutch computer scientist demonstrated that identities can be forged. Although it did not turn out to be a criminal business case yet, it does show how important it is to involve these experts from the start before actual criminals catch up and do real damage. Concerning marketing, the Dutch case is also interesting. While JR East refrains from marketing, as it is perceived as offensive, Dutch transport companies pushed the edges of the law. This resulted in an opt-out for travel products and an opt-in for other advertisements, only by the transport company who provided the product. This is now also clearly stated in their privacy statement. If people want to opt for anonymity, it has its price. While travellers in Hong Kong can opt for an anonymous Octopus subscription as 'elder', 'youngster' or 'student', the Dutch OV-chip card only provides discounts on a personalised basis. Finally, some cases of police investigation occurred in all these systems, but only in case of individual suspects of severe crime.

It remains to be seen if these travel data will also be used for data mining for suspicious profiles or petty crime.

One important omission in the Dutch approach is user empowerment. What do travellers gain from all this? Their 16-digit identity could have served all sorts of purposes. Payment is not made easier; rather, more difficult. People forget to check out and end up paying more. Season card holders, who could previously just take a seat, now also have to check in and out. Using the card for other transactions, like in the Asian systems, is still not possible. A best pricing system (e.g. automatic subscription and travelling free of charge after a number of similar trips) was once promised, but is currently far away. Getting a full on-line overview of all your trips, for example for invoices, has only recently become possible. Finally, providing an on-line overview of travel congestion for enabling travellers to decide on their best travel behaviour may just remain a mere future vision. This will only occur once the whole nation has shifted to one system that works. It is an open question whether it ever will.

13
.TAG

Will all Dutch stations be gated, or not?

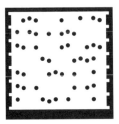

TAG for note 12

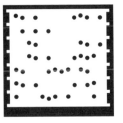

TAG for note 13

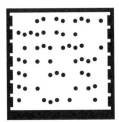

TAG for note 18

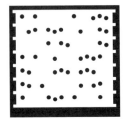

TAG for note 19

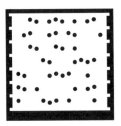

TAG for note 25

Notes

1. http://www.octopus.com.hk/octopus-for-businesses/benefits-for-your-business/en/index.html
2. JR East Press Release, http://www.jreast.co.jp/press/2009/20091014.pdf
3. Interviews by Christian van 't Hof with Pedro Peters (28 May 2008), director of RET and Peter van Dijk (10 June 2009), director of Mcom.
4. Correspondence with Janniek Zandee from TLS.
5. Organisations for travellers such as ROVER, Fietserbond and ANWB; consumer affairs such as the Consumentenbond, and special interest groups such as the elderly, handicapped and those with chronic illness.
6. Broek, S. van den & N. Radewalt (26 March 2009). Evaluatie OV-chipkaart. Roelofarendsveen: DocAdvies, p. 5.
7. 'Klachtenregen over OV-chipkaart' rtl, 26 October 2010.
8. Questions raised in Parliament by member Mastwijk (CDA) on 7 september 2009 to the Secretary of State Huizinga.
9. http://www.leiden.pvda.nl/nieuws/nieuws_item/i/3398/t/weg_met_de_poortjes
10. Winter, B. de (7 November 2008). 'CBP sluit privacy-deal met NS over OV-chipkaart.' On: Webwereld.nl
11. 'De OV-chipkaart en uw persoonsgegevens' (16 September 2009), http://www.ov-chipkaart.nl/pdf/22246/ovchipenuwpersoonsgegevens
12. Schilpzand, W. & C. van 't Hof (2008). RFID as the Key to the Ubiquitous Network Society. A Japanese Case Study on Identity Management. The Hague: Rathenau Institute.
13. Wouter Teepe, during 'De OV-chipshow', organised by the Rathenau Institute and Tumult, Utrecht 19 May 2008.
14. Broek, P. van den (2008). 'De schokgolf na de ontmanteling'. In: VOX, 8, no. 15, pp.14-18.
15. Idem.
16. Huizinga, T. (28 november 2008). Actualisatie Aanvalsplan OV-chipkaart, pp. 7, 8.
17. Personal communication Christian van 't Hof with Jaap Henk Hoepman and Wouter Teepe from the Digital Security Group.
18. https://ovchip.cs.ru.nl/Main_Page
19. Gaby Hinsliff In: The Observer (Sunday 16 March 2008).
20. Idem Schilpzand, W. & C. van 't Hof (2008).
21. Decision by the Rotterdam Court on 2 June 2008, filed under 07/956.
22. Idem Schilpzand, W. & C. van 't Hof (2008).
23. Broek, S. van den & N. Radewalt (26 March 2009). Evaluatie OV-chipkaart. Roelofarendsveen: DocAdvies.
24. AD 26 October 2010, 'Klachtensite ov-chipkaart staat roodgloeiend'.
25. Heuvel, E. van den et al. (2007). 'RFID-bewustzijn van consumenten: Hoe denken Nederlanders over Radio Frequency Identification?' A survey by the Rathenau Institute, Consumentenbond and ECP.NL.
26. Idem Heuvel, E. van den et al. (2007).

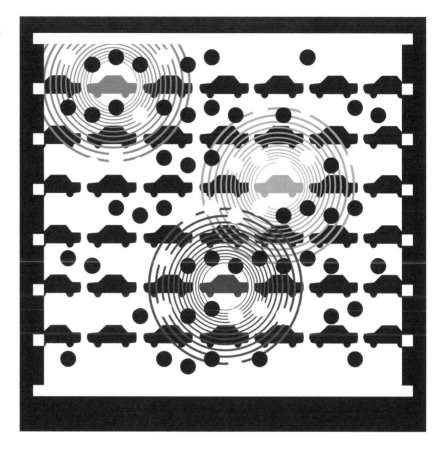

Case 0010

Networked Cars

Christian van 't Hof, Rinie van Est
and Selene Kolman

'People are willing to be tracked, as long as there is something in return and they have a choice.'

Towards a Digitalised Road Network

For long, automobiles were isolated vehicles that drove around on roads. However, many Dutch cars are currently equipped with mobile telecommunication, satellite navigation and sensors, turning them into driving computers. Meanwhile, the roads, too, are being digitalised. Sensors, antennas and cameras track vehicles for traffic management, security and, eventually, dynamic road pricing. The automobile becomes a moving, networked terminal.

How is the identity of cars and their drivers managed in digitalising Dutch road networks? We will first describe how the Dutch government has tried to implement dynamic road pricing, making use of different technological options to get cars into the network, and failed. We then turn to businesses that did succeed in getting cars on-line and how they have been managing their identities. The section on the future of network cars sketches some public-private partnerships that lay ahead and IdM issues that still need to be resolved.

This case study shows how important it is to take anonymity as a default setting; not only to protect privacy, but also to empower drivers. Data on moving vehicles gathered by both governments and businesses can be reused to inform drivers on the situation on the road, as long as the data is disconnected from specific persons or vehicles. It also demonstrates that people are willing to be tracked, as long as there is something in return and they have a choice in the kind of system they use.

0010 Governments Connecting
.0001 Cars to the Net

According to the Dutch Mobility Act (2004), mobility is 'an achievement which provides people the opportunity to develop themselves and relax'. This achievement will also cause fatalities, congestion, environmental damage and noise.[1] Traffic jams are seen as a big burden: economically, socially and ecologically. Meanwhile, road traffic is also an important source of income for the state, as only part of the billions of taxes are used for road maintenance. The question of how to balance an individual need for mobility with the collective costs and benefits has triggered fierce debates over the last decades. Just building more roads has not proven to be the final solution: it just attracts more traffic. Dynamic road pricing is therefore seen as one of the solutions. You pay as you drive: more if it is rush hour or if you are on busy roads, less if there is space available. As sound as this principle may be, it has proven to be difficult to implement in practice.

0010 How the Dutch government failed
.0001 to implement dynamic road pricing
.0001

Many congested cities have adopted this principle for their traffic management. One of the frontrunners was Singapore. Toll ports were already implemented in 1975 and they were replaced by electronic versions in 1998. Cars were equipped with a RFID chip from which readers deduct a payment according to the road and time of day. This system is comparable to the French Liber-T system which was implemented in 2005. London is a particular example: the congestion charge programme, dating from 2003, also has the aim to prevent traffic jams by dynamic pricing, but uses automatic number plate recognition. Hereby, not only the car, but also its owner is identified.

In the Netherlands, the idea of dynamic road pricing ('rekeningrijden' or 'kilometerheffing') started in 1987, when minister of Transport Smit-Kroes predicted this new, fair system would be implemented in 1995. Succeeding minsters May-Weggen (1989-1994), Jorritsma (1994-1998), Netelenbos (1998-2002), Peijs (2003-2007), as well as Eurlings (2007-2010), were all enthusiastic about the idea, pushed it forward in a myriad of ways and even implemented some bills on dynamic road pricing. Still, all failed to implement it.

In order to calculate the price for use of the road, cars need to be tracked. When minister Jorritsma proposed to equip big cities with toll ports, the Data Protection Agency filed a protest. The system would register

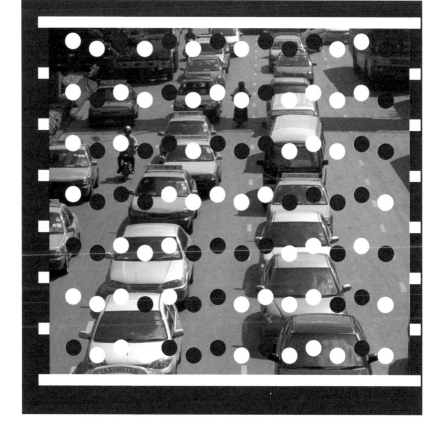

where and when someone would enter the payment zone, which is seen as an unnecessary infringement on the privacy of the car owner. The DPA therefore stipulated that the following principle must apply: electronic road charges should be as anonymous as cash payments.[2]

One of the first pilot projects dates back to 1999 and was started by minister Netelenbos. Inspired by the Singapore system, Dutch cars would carry electronic prepaid cards and readers would deduct five guilders once they drove into a big city in the morning. This system could have

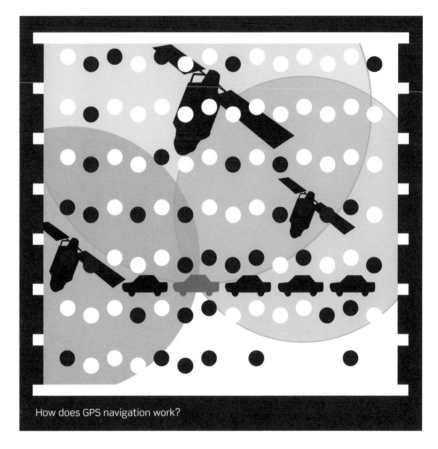

How does GPS navigation work?

been anonymous in principle, but it had a catch. If a chip wouldn't have enough credit, the car's number plate would be scanned and a bill would be sent automatically to the owner. This again let to privacy concerns. The DPA claimed this system would probably not only be used for its original purpose. Meanwhile the ANWB (Royal Dutch Touring Club, an association that represents most car owners in the Netherlands), joined ranks and turned it into an economic issue. According to its director Paul Nouwen, the new system would only lead to 'Paying while you wait in a traffic jam'.[3] After the ANWB campaign 'Stop rekeningrijden!' ('Stop road pricing!'), the system was left off the agenda for a while.

Meanwhile traffic jams in the Netherlands increased and environmental concerns gained prominence on the political agenda. The next minster, Peijs, established alliances with environmental organisations, and the car lobby and successfully passed the bill 'Anders betalen voor mobiliteit' ('Different Payment for Mobility') in the Dutch Parliament in 2005. In this bill the idea of toll ports was replaced by a registration box in the car with GPS tracking.[4] It paved the way for the serious implementation of dynamic road pricing for the next minister, Camile Eurling, who has been an outspoken enthusiast about the idea.

Eurlings developed a plan based on the 'Pay as you drive' principle and sent it to Parliament in October 2009. Road pricing would be differentiated by time, place and the characteristics of each car in question and fully implemented by 2018. Cars would not only be tracked for payment, but also for traffic management, for example by predicting congestion and informing drivers about it. The plan also involved public transport. Combining a national database on road traffic with one on public transport, both the government, as well as businesses and citizens, would gain a full overview of mobility in the Netherlands, which would lead to more intelligent mobility behaviour. An ambitious plan indeed, but Eurlings forgot one thing: paragraph 9.2 on privacy only mentioned it (the paragraph) needs to be filled in later on...[5] This is because he had not yet decided on the kind of system that would be used.

Since Eurlings' plans were revealed, the responses in Dutch newspapers and Parliament ranged from cynicism to outrage. Some political parties even proposed to hold a referendum, to have the citizens decide on it. Then, at the beginning of 2010, the already critical ANWB announced a survey amongst their members concerning the plan for dynamic road pricing. Although the questionnaire did not produce a simple 'yes' or 'no' verdict for the plan, but rather an inventory of arguments for or against it, minister Eurlings immediately announced that the continuation of his plans would depend on the outcome of the survey. It turned out that 68 per cent agreed on the principle 'pay as you drive', but a large majority was negative about the way that the scheme would be executed, especially about the way in which driving behaviour would be registered. The figures showed that most people feared that the new system would be too expensive and that they had no guarantees their privacy would be sufficiently protected.[6] Meanwhile, the Dutch government has fallen. The implementation of the registration box in the car awaits yet another minister; or it may just vanish from the political agenda.

0010 .0001 .0010 Many IdM issues remain unresolved

There are two versions of the 'box in the car': a 'thin' and a 'thick' one. With the thin version, the registration box continuously sends a signal to the administration office, which then calculates the costs for driving based on distance, time, type of road, and so on. To protect the driver's privacy, specific locations and time are encrypted and not sent to the government. As drivers are being tracked live, they can receive location-based information from service providers. With this thin version, a driver can disable it by jamming the signal, but this can be checked by law enforcers. With the thick version, the calculation is performed inside the box and the result is periodically sent to the administration office. In this version, the driver can travel anonymously, but the box provides fewer services and it is probably more expensive. Fraud with the thick version is technically more difficult, but also more difficult to prove.

Without a clear choice on whether the thin or thick administration system will be used and who is going to build and maintain it, privacy issues remain unresolved. According to the Data Protection Agency, the thick version may be more privacy friendly, as no specific time and location data is gathered by the administration office. It also provides drivers with a record of proof, in case the administration office makes a mistake. Still, this version is more expensive and less likely to be chosen if commercial companies will implement the system: they will want to track their customers for location-based services. To secure privacy in case the thin version is chosen, the administrator could calculate the cost and store this instead of the time and location data. Still, drivers then have to trust that this is done correctly, as there will be no record to check it.

Also, there are many questions on the data security of the system. Security expert Bart Jacobs states this nation wide system, which involves so much money, will be a true hacker's trophy. Mobility expert Huitema from IBM, one of the possible suppliers of the system, claims that 'the security of our system is comparable to the security standards of the US Army'. According to Rietveld, security expert at Traxion, any system will have to deal with leaks in the mobile communication networks. GSM, GPRS and UMTS all have security holes we still cannot fix. Also, the protocols of the GPS interface are far from secure.

Finally, it remains unclear to what extent police officers may use traffic management systems for law enforcement. The organisation which collects data for traffic management, the RDW (Rijksdienst Wegverkeer), is currently building a live map of all roads with a collection of anonymous dots. Will it be made compatible with identification systems such as the Automatic Number Plate Registration system, turning the dots into identified vehicles? Will the box in the car be treated like a mobile phone and therefore fall under the current data retention directive? Will administration offices be obliged to keep all data on which vehicle has been where and when, in case the police need it for investigation purposes? Or will law enforcement simply make do with current systems already at hand, such as the ANPR and speed cameras?

0010 Businesses Succeed in
.0010 Connecting Cars to the Net

Meanwhile, businesses have succeeded in connecting cars to the net. They did so at first by applying the governmental Global Positioning System to civil purposes and developing car navigation devices. Next, they added mobile phone technology for informing drivers through the same box, as well as to track cars and predict flows of traffic. Identity Management issues seem to be resolved by tracking cars only through anonymous data and by leaving personalisation as an option. This system works so well that it has drawn the attention of the Dutch government, who aim to use the data from these businesses for traffic management instead of their own.

0010 How companies reuse governmental and
.0010 personal data to empower customers
.0001

GPS consists of 24 satellites orbiting the earth, each broadcasting their own unique signal. If a navigation device catches at least four signals, it's able to locate the position with an accuracy of a few metres. This position can be plotted on a digital road map, providing real-time location information. In this case, the car is not connected, it is merely receiving signals. A connection is made possible through the mobile phone network, i.e. by adding a SIM card, a processor and antennas to the car and by hooking it up to the GPRS or GSM network. In this way, the car is not only receiving, but also returning data.

GPS navigation was first applied in the US Military, with a distorted signal to secure for defence use only. In May 2000, the US government freed it up for commercial use, triggering a whole host of companies that provide navigation to all vehicles. It started in logistics, where freight and business vehicles were equipped with navigation and a network connection that supported not only their drivers, but it was also used for fleet management. Next came the high-end consumer vehicles, such as BMW's 'ConnectedDrive', dripping down to the lower segments, through either built-in or add-on navigation devices. A staggering growth in sales proves there is a huge market for car navigation.

The world's leading provider of location and navigation devices is currently TomTom. Headquartered in The Netherlands, this company has over 3,000 employees worldwide. In 2009, TomTom reported €1.5 billion in revenues, a €340 million net cash flow from operating activities, and over 45 million people use their products every day.[7] Simon Hania from TomTom claims the most important technological trend currently is 'connecting the car as real-time as possible'.[8] His company therefore aligned with Vodafone in 2007 to form Traffic Data Service. This is a clearing house for all sorts of data gathered on the road from phone signals, cameras and sensors, for the purpose of generating a real-time image of what happens on the road. It also uses computer models to predict traffic based on speed profiles from the past.

Central to the real-time image are the so-called Timing Advance Reports which TomTom receives from Vodafone. These reports state which mobile phone is connected to which antenna in which area as well as the strength of the signal that received. If someone in a moving car makes a phone call, it can be calculated where the vehicle is located and how fast it driving. Through aggregating data on a number of vehicles, traffic jams can be located or even predicted. Subscribers to the TomTom HD Traffic service get this real-time image of road traffic on their navigation device through the GPRS network. It also provides safety warnings, weather forecasts, fuel prices and local search engines powered by Google. At the time of writing, over a million users throughout the world subscribed to this service, using the fused data from 80 million mobile phone handsets. This TomTom driving community generates 22 million kilometres of high definition road coverage in Europe, the Americas, South Africa and Asia-Pacific.[9]

TNO, a renowned Dutch technology research institute, shows that car navigation has a number of positive effects. The technology helps to bring down the travel distance and time and saves fuel and other costs. Navigation also has a positive effect on safety: the device heightens the attention of the driver, while it lowers stress on being lost.[10] From the perspective of empowerment, the benefits therefore seem clear. But how about privacy, especially for those who are tracked without gaining the benefits because they don't posses a car navigator? What kind of personal data do Vodafone and TomTom use from people? How well is the right to driving anonymously protected?

People who subscribe to TomTom HD Traffic fall under the telecom services law and the Dutch Data Protection Act. These laws state personal data can only be used once the user has given informed consent, which is covered in their Licence Term Agreement. To prevent unauthorised use of the on-board data, Trip logs are encrypted. TomTom also cuts off the beginning and end of the trip, so it cannot be traced to a specific address. To secure the privacy of other road users, Vodafone separates the Timing Advance Reports from any identification numbers of the phone (phone number, IMEI, SIM, etc.). Instead, vehicles are given a random number, which also changes every hour. TomTom only needs to know how many cars are driving on a particular road and at what speed, not who is in the cars. Therefore, only customers who want to be known are identified; others stay anonymous.[11]

0010 .0010 .0010 Public-private traffic management

Up until now, traffic management in the Netherlands has been a top-down model, based on sensors and cameras on the road. Counting the numbers of vehicles and measuring their speed, the Ministry of Transport has been trying to steer the flow of traffic by changing speed limits, warnings and access to roads. With the rise of networked navigation, traffic management is complemented by a bottom-up approach: through drivers adjusting their driving behaviour according to their live map. These two approaches form the basis for a new organisation: the National Data Warehouse for Traffic Information. This organisation will collect, process, store and distribute all relevant traffic data. According to its director Marja van Strien, 80 per cent of data currently comes from the conventional governmental sensors and cameras, and 20 per cent comes from navigation providers such as TomTom. Soon, the ratio will be the reverse.[12]

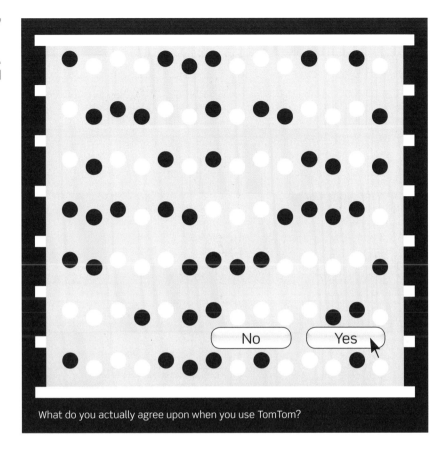

What do you actually agree upon when you use TomTom?

Data will be plotted on Google Maps in order to provide a live image of road traffic. The main highways are already covered. The aim is to fully cover all roads in the Netherlands by 2015. This map will also contain data from public transport. Travellers can then decide whether the train or the car fits their particular needs. This way, mobility will be based on well-informed travellers instead of centralised steering. Van Strien is very principled about the use of the traffic data: it only contains the amount, speed and location of vehicles and claims this is the only way the system will be accepted. No one can or will be identified through the system, and therefore options for road taxing or law enforcement are excluded in the architecture of the system.

Connecting your car to the net

What kinds of devices do we see in cars? What kinds of identification numbers are attached to us and our vehicles? Through which networks do they form a digital identity? From within the car, our mobile phones provide a unique number to the network from our SIM card and IMEI number, and this identifies the device in the mobile network (GSM, GPRS, UMTS or WIMAX). Navigation devices can be networked using the same technology. If they are not connected, they can be hooked up to the internet at home on our computer, uploading our trip logs to the provider. In case of TomTom, this data is encrypted, and the starting position and destination of the trips are cut off. The account for logging on to MyTomTom requires a name, sex and residence. Other personal data are requested but not mandatory. Besides our phone and navigation, the eCall system can also be connected through the mobile network: in case of a car crash it automatically dials 112 for emergency services.[13]

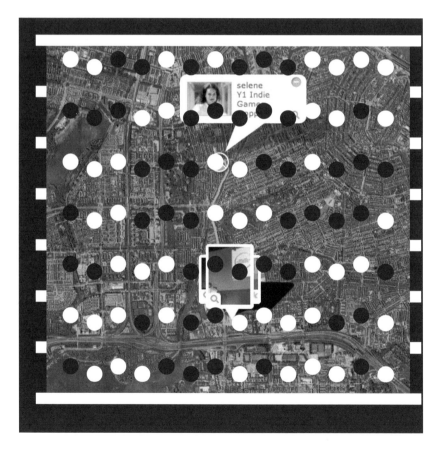

18
.TAG

Around the car, there are also a number of tracking devices. First of all, the 24 satellites forming the GPS system each provide a unique signal which is received by our navigation device. The satellites don't track us; we track them. Nevertheless, the GPS coordinates can be sent to others, using the mobile networks. Antennas for mobile communication track both mobile phones as well as connected navigation devices. Their unique numbers can be used for the administration of the mobile network operator. When used for traffic overviews, devices receive a random number each hour.

This function is also performed by sensors in the road and cameras next to the road. Different kinds of cameras and sensors are placed for speed control and are able to scan number plates. These data are managed by the police. Finally, number plates can also be read by ordinary citizens. On-line (through the internet or an SMS service), such a number can reveal the age, value and technical specifications of any given car.

0010 .0011 Conclusions

Over the last years the Dutch road system has been turned into a network of connected cars. Mobility has thereby become an Identity Management issue. One could wonder why the government failed in getting the cars connected while companies succeeded in just a matter of five years. TomTom has proven that people are willing to pay and be tracked if it increases their mobility. Vodafone has demonstrated how traffic can be monitored without tracking people, using random numbers instead of personal data. Taking anonymity as the default setting, data can be reused to inform drivers, which demonstrates that privacy and empowerment can actually go hand in hand.

The government, meanwhile, has demonstrated serious flaws in Identity Management. It remains unclear what the system would actually register and what the data will be used for, and citizens remain unconvinced on what they would actually gain from this system. However, the organisations representing drivers, such as ANWB and DPA appear to be powerful enough to stifle the process. This is typical for the Dutch 'polder culture': there is one technological system for coping with all problems, which is decided on by everyone – just like with building dikes.

A fundamental difference between car navigation and dynamic road taxing is choice. Drivers can choose whether they use car navigation or not, and they can select their own provider. With road taxing, it seems to be a one-off solution for everyone and this upsets drivers. But perhaps if the government allows different systems to evolve side by side, one of them will prove to be the best solution – a system that both empowers drivers with more mobility and protects their privacy as they drive their networked car.

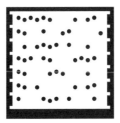

TAG for note 1

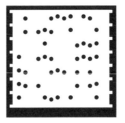

TAG for note 6

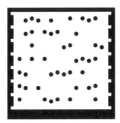

TAG for note 7

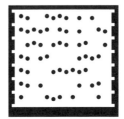

TAG for note 9

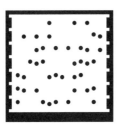

TAG for note 13

Notes

1 Ministerie van Verkeer en Waterstaat (2004). 'Nota Mobiliteit: naar een betrouwbare en voorspelbare bereikbaarheid', p. 16.

2 Registratiekamer (18 December 1997). 'Rekening rijden bedreigt anonimiteit weggebruiker. Registratiekamer bekritiseert wetsvoorstel'.

3 Van de Sande, J. & F. van Straaten. 'Botsing over rekeningrijden'. In: NRC Handelsblad, 17 April 1999.

4 Saris, C.M. & A. Drahmann (2008). 'De Wet bereikbaarheid en mobiliteit in vogelvlucht'. In: Bouwrecht 4, no. 48, pp. 225-233.

5 Consultatieversie memorie van toelichting Wet kilometerprijs, 23 July 2008. (3) De betalingsplicht, 3.4.3, p. 34.

6 Ruigrok Netpanel (2010), 'Samenvatting Ledenpeiling kilometerprijs. Een kwantitatief en kwalitatief online onderzoek naar de opvattingen over het wetsontwerp Kilometerprijs. In opdracht van de ANWB'.

7 Company profile on tomtom.com, 14 September 2010.

8 Interview by Selene Kolman (13 August 2009) with Simon Hania, Senior Vice President Publishing, Dynamic Content & Publishing TomTom.

9 'One million connected drivers enjoy world's most accurate traffic service'. Press release by TomTom 2 September 2010.

10 TNO (2007). 'Onafhankelijk onderzoek toont aan dat navigatiesystemen een positieve invloed hebben op verkeersveiligheid'.

11 Interview by Selene Koolman (13 augustus 2009) with Simon Hania, Senior Vice President Publishing, Dynamic Content & Publishing TomTom.

12 Interview by Selene Kolman and Christian van 't Hof (3 September 2009) with Marja van Strien, director of National Data Warehouse for Traffic Information.

13 European Commission, DG Information Society (July 2010) 'eCall – saving lives through in-vehicle communication technology'.

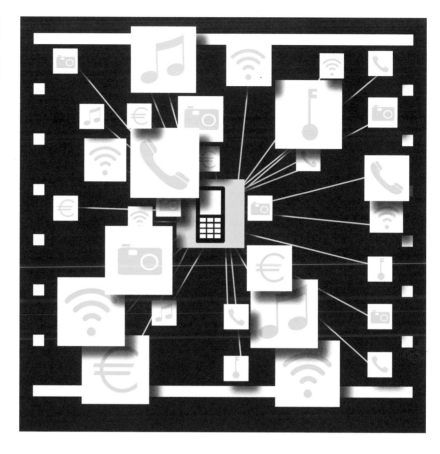

Case 0011

Money Mobiles

Wouter Schilpzand, Christian van 't Hof
and Bart Schermer

'NFC turns your mobile

into a mouse to click

on icons in digitalised

public space.'

How NFC Can Turn Your Mobile Phone into a Wallet, Key and Identity Manager

The days are long gone that a mobile phone was just a device that could make phone calls. We use it to communicate in text and speech, update our calendar, send email, browse the web and navigate from A to B. One next move in the evolution of the mobile phone is to integrate it with that other vital item in our pocket: the wallet. This vision has driven the development of Near Field Communication (NFC). NFC is a technology that can transform a mobile phone into a wallet, a key or even a mouse with which one can click in public space for information.

This case study contrasts two innovation trajectories for two similar applications: the global NFC and FeliCa in Japan. NFC demonstrates how difficult it is in an open market to agree on how this technology should function, let alone to agree on how identities should be managed. Who keeps track of our identities? How does a profile emerge when consistently using NFC to unlock information and services? At the same time, the openness of this technology demonstrates new possibilities for user empowerment, as it enables them to manage their identity themselves.

On the other hand, Mobile FeliCa in Japan was developed as a closed, proprietary system by one company: FeliCa Networks, which developed both the technology and the services and manages the identities of its users. While NFC is still in its infancy, FeliCa is currently integrated in half of all Japanese mobile phones and part of daily life in the public space.

NFC is RFID in your mobile

Near Field Communication is based on the same RFID technology that is used in smart cards for contactless payment, or for access, like with the Japanese Mobile FeliCa card, London's Oyster Card or the OV-Chipkaart in the Netherlands (see case study *Gated Stations*). It operates on the same 13.56 MHz frequency band and uses the same principle of proximity (contactless communication within a range of approximately 10 centimetres). The big difference with the 'standard' RFID smart cards is that NFC acts as both a chip and a reader: it can also be used to read other NFC tags.

The NFC chip is designed for integration in devices such as mobiles. It doesn't have a user interface of its own, but relies on the keyboard and screen of your mobile for users to manage the NFC applications. Because NFC equipped phones can act both as a tag and as a reader, there are three ways in which it functions: as a smart card (e.g., for payment or access), for access to digital content (reading NFC tags embedded in the environment) and for the exchange of data (similar to Bluetooth) between NFC enabled devices.

0011 Money Mobiles
.0001 around the World

We can currently distinguish three innovation trajectories for mobile payment. Most successful in terms of the number of users is the Mobile FeliCa in Japan. Near Field Communication is a global development, with many players and conflicting interests. Finally, Chinese state-led companies are aiming to set their own standards, but they have not yet succeeded. These different innovation trajectories not only determine the rate of user adoption, but also lead to different Identity Management issues.

0011
.0001 Mobile FeliCa
.0001

Mobile FeliCa technology is developed and managed by FeliCa Networks, a joint venture of Japan's leading Mobile Network Operator NTT DoCoMo, Sony and JR East, Japan's largest railway company. Introduced in 2004, it is mainly used for payments (both as a personal debit card and as an anonymous cash replacement), as a transit card for public transport in the Tokyo area, and as a loyalty card. The Japanese therefore call it *osaifu keitai*, or 'money mobile'. Its introduction went quite smoothly, as these big companies set up one joined venture to deliver both the technology and services, agreed on standards and reached a critical mass of users. By October 2009, about 60 million of the mobile phones in use in Japan were equipped with the Mobile FeliCa technology, which was half of the total Japanese mobile phone market.[1]

FeliCa Networks is the single point where all data generated by FeliCa Mobiles is managed. For most Mobile FeliCa applications, they also host service providers' databases, distribute applications and manage the portfolios of clients. The identity of Mobile FeliCa users is therefore managed by one single party that users and providers can refer to. In practice, this means, for example, that if you want to switch phones or if you lose your phone with all its applications, you can retrieve a copy of your settings at FeliCa Networks.

0011 NFC
.0001
.0010

The development of NFC did not go as smoothly as was the case with Mobile FeliCa. Contrary to the proprietary Mobile FeliCa technology, NFC is developed as an open system. Competitors meet at the international NFC Forum, the institution overseeing NFC standardisation and promoting its use. As this forum grew over the years, internal tension arose amongst its members, as different groups of actors sought to pursue different goals through NFC.

The main conflict revolved around the location of the Secure Element (SE): the tamperproof chip on which sensitive information is stored. In the one corner, Mobile Network Operators (MNOs) congregated, united under the banner of the GSM Association. They aimed to appropriate the SE and have it placed on the phone's SIM card, which is under their control. This would allow MNOs to charge NFC service providers a fee for making use of the SIM. Other options for SE placement are embedding it in the mobile itself or placing it on an external memory card. The service providers, most vocally represented by banks, opted for the placement in the handset itself or on an external memory card, as it would allow them more freedom in using NFC than by partnering with the MNOs.

While no formal statement has been made about the NFC Forum's position on where the SE will be located, standards organisation ETSI has codified placing the SE on the SIM as a standard. Nokia has announced that their future NFC models will be compatible with this standard, suggesting that this conflict has ended in the favour of the GSM Association.[2] Embedding this vital part of NFC technology in on a proprietary chip creates the danger of lock-in effects: NFC service would be intrinsically linked to your MNO. If you switch your phone subscription, you may lose your NFC services and if you have an MNO with no NFC services, you will be unable to get it any other way. Furthermore, if MNOs pursue their intentions of charging fees for use of the SE, this could hamper the development of new services.

At the same time, while the standards were being finalised, another problem arose: where were the NFC phones? Manufacturers like Nokia and Samsung, both members of the NFC Forum, hesitated to mass-produce NFC handsets, as hardly any services existed. Potential service providers, on the other hand, needed people to have NFC in their mobiles to start offering services. While this chicken-and-egg problem still exists, it may

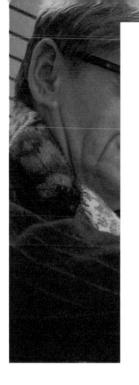

20
.TAG

be resolved shortly; at the time of writing, Nokia, the first manufacturer to make NFC mobiles available on a commercial scale, has indicated to equip most smart phones with NFC from the end of 2010.[3] Another break-through could come from Apple, which has started hiring senior staff with NFC experience and taken out patents on the integration of RFID into iPhones and on setting up NFC services.

0011 .0001 .0011 China Mobile

This comparison between FeliCa and NFC does not necessary mean that a closed off, centralised innovation model is better than an open one. In China, for example, the market of over one billion handheld devices is dominated by one state-led company: China Mobile. This provider ran some trials with payment systems at vending machines. As they integrated the NFC read/write chip into the SIM card, they used the 2.4 GHz band. This high frequency was seen as necessary in order to get through to the device, but also made the device too sensitive to skimming and hacking. Moreover, it made mobiles incompatible with applications on the 13.56 MHz contactless technology, such as public transport payment systems.[4] Finally, it was unclear whether China Mobile was allowed to work as a bank. Currently, China Union (which proceeds all payments), China Telecom and some other operators are joining the game and looking for collaboration.[5] Perhaps in future, the Chinese may get their mobile payment too.

0011 .0010 Implementing NFC in the Dynamic Dutch Market

The Dutch mobile market is an interesting test case for NFC: almost everyone uses a mobile phone (there are more mobile phones than inhabitants), there is a fierce competition between different providers, and people switch handsets and providers quite frequently. In this dynamic market, many NFC trials were held, but none reached full implementation. The most elaborate pilots held with NFC in the Netherlands revolved around two systems: Payter and Rabo Mobiel. Both started in 2007 and both experimented with a diverse range of NFC functions, while centring on payment. From these failed attempts we can draw some lessons on Identity Management in NFC.

0011 Payter
.0010
.0001

Payter equipped a shopping district in Rotterdam with NFC payment terminals and furnished users with a Nokia 6131-NFC. By accessing the Payter application, users could transfer money to their Payter account, which acted as their mobile wallet with which they could buy items in participating stores. Spending money in the Payter wallet would earn users Tsjings, Payter's own loyalty scheme. Smart posters in a supermarket could be tapped for shopping lists associated with the menu on the poster. From time to time, coupons could be downloaded for special offers. Payter grew to offer access to parking, cinema tickets and payment in over a hundred shops and restaurants to its 1400 users.

   The role that Payter saw for itself was a spider in a web of services and consumers that made use of the Payter system: other service providers were invited to make use of Payter's system to offer their services. Payter saw the mobile wallet as a way to connect consumers and advertisers in a meaningful way. However, it never came to that. As 2008 drew to a close, Payter aimed to expand their services to six other cities in The Netherlands. To help persuade retailers, they offered the payment terminals for free. The move failed, as retailers mistrusted Payter's intentions. Thus, Payter remained a Rotterdam exclusive. One year later, in December 2009, Payter announced that they would stop running the system and instead focus on developing back-end systems for others to implement.

0011 Rabo Mobiel
.0010
.0010

The second system was spearheaded by Rabo Mobiel, a subsidiary of the Rabobank, one of the largest banks in the Netherlands. Banks have an entirely different motivation for introducing NFC. Handling and producing cash costs 84 billion Euros a year in Europe alone.[6] Using cards or mobile phones to virtualise transactions is a means to cut these costs. Furthermore, mobile payment provides banks with an opportunity to interact with their clients more regularly. As banks rely on trust as their main asset, the implementation of Rabo Mobiel's pilots was more modest in terms both of speed and scale. Instead of creating an entire system in one go, they carefully held a number of separate pilots in order to learn how to apply the new technology, study user response and build a network of potential partners to work with.

   The earlier pilots were very brief and lasted only a day. Over time, the trials became more elaborate. Perhaps the best example was a six-month pilot in a supermarket. 100 customers in that supermarket received an NFC mobile that took the function of their debit card. Participants, instead of swiping the bankcard, tapped their mobile before validating the transaction through entering a PIN code. As an added function, the deposit on glass bottles was returned using NFC. Participants could choose to either subtract the amount from their bill, or give it to charity. Users felt positive about this new way of paying. Even older people, who thus far had not used mobile phones, indicated finding the service useful.

A similar pilot in another supermarket that should have led to a permanent service with nationwide coverage ended prematurely, as the worldwide financial crisis set in and Rabobank needed its resources elsewhere. They effectively suspended all innovation carried out at Rabo Mobiel.

Next steps for NFC

At the end of 2008, Dutch experts[7] indicated that NFC had left its pilot phase and that the technology was ready for permanent introduction. As a result of many factors, amongst which the global recession, no services have been introduced since Payter and Rabo Mobiel. However, in September 2010, three Dutch banks and three Dutch MNOs issued a statement[8] that they are once again working on creating a system for mobile payment, to be introduced at an unspecified date in the future.

As the struggle between different stakeholders within the standardisation process for NFC clearly illustrates, an important step for the further development of NFC is the cooperation between different stakeholders. The establishment of a Trusted Service Manager (TSM), a third party that ensures that all the different kinds of hardware and all the different kinds

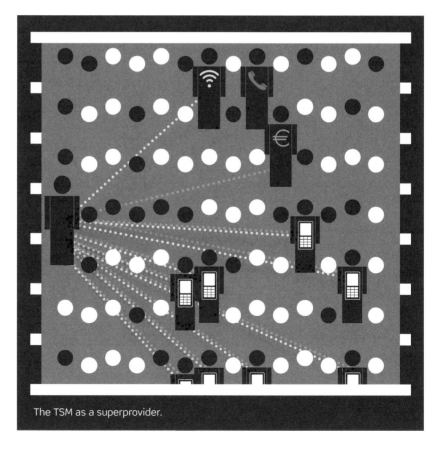

The TSM as a superprovider.

of services get connected through NFC, could prove a useful element in an NFC ecosystem. From the user perspective, too, a TSM can play an important part. Just like FeliCa Networks, the TSM could store a copy of a user's applications and their data, so that when they switch phones or in case of theft or loss, they get quick access to their mobile wallet again. Furthermore, a TSM can ensure that NFC will be developed as an open system with room for services that empower users or even for user generated applications, rather than as a bundle of proprietary environments where users are locked in. However, with the hopes of a smooth NFC rollout in 2008, the urgency for establishing a TSM disappeared. There is little evidence that these negotiations have been resumed.

0011 With NFC, Your Identity
.0011 is Managed by Many or None...

In case of FeliCa and China Mobile, one single provider could set the standards, implement the technology and develop services accordingly. For the user it is clear who is managing their identity, but it is difficult for other companies to join the game and add new services. In the development of NFC technology, a diverse range of actors has been involved. Similarly, in developing NFC services, many different organisations will tinker with this technology. How are our digital identities managed and who is in control? A Trusted Service Manager may be needed, not only as an intermediary between competing providers, but also as a single point where legislation on data storage can be enforced and to which users can turn in case something goes wrong.

Every NFC transaction yields data on your behaviour, whether you retrieve information, conduct payments, get access or collect points. Data on the time, date, nature and place of the transaction is stored in the service providers' databases. This will result in the creation of rich user profiles that can be analysed and acted upon. It is potentially beneficial for everyone, as it allows tailored and meaningful services, but it also brings risks. With service providers getting such an elaborate insight into the behaviour of users, the risk exists that an asymmetrical division of information gives service providers possibilities for influencing user behaviour, and thus a measure of control over the individual. Furthermore, careless use, misuse and even abuse of personal data may harm the individual. Therefore, it is highly recommended that databases on different functions within the same service are kept separate or made separable in order to minimise adverse effects like information asymmetries and data misuse.

The rich profiles are not just of interest to commercial parties. Law enforcement is more than likely to take an interest if NFC data if it can help in solving crimes. For instance, NFC can be used as evidence in criminal cases (e.g. evidence of who checked in with his NFC phone at this terminal between 8 and 9 in the evening). NFC data can also be used pro-actively for data mining and automated profiling. Data retention laws apply here (see first chapter), but it remains unclear how exactly they apply. Can NFC providers comply with these directives? What does it cost them to store, structure and provide these data? This remains unclear.

Finally, what opportunities do users have to manage their identity themselves? For instance, in the pilots we witnessed, service providers offer users the opportunity to access to their own transaction history, giving them a greater degree of insight into the use of their personal data. Furthermore, users can be given choices in the level of protection of applications. Also, new services, such as the Privacy Coach, can increase user empowerment. To allow such services to be developed, it is important that NFC develops as an open and transparent system.

Privacy Coach turns phone into Identity Manager

RFID is increasingly used in smart cards and to tag products. In many cases, this led to privacy concerns.[9] If you pay or check in with a smart card, or purchase a tagged product, what does the provider actually register of you? The Dutch Ministry of Economic Affairs therefore investigated the possibilities a system of logos, each stating what kind of personal data was registered using tags, but this proved to be impractical. The Dutch Interdisciplinary Forum on RFID (DIFR) therefore took a very different approach: using a NFC phone to check on tags.

This so-called Privacy Coach works as follows.[10] One first sets a privacy profile by answering a set of questions, for example, 'would you allow tagged product sales to build up an anonymous customer profile?'

or, 'would you allow a the card to register when you enter a building?'. For example, if the person becomes a member of a fitness club and receives an access card, he can scan the new card with his phone. The provider of the card has filled in the same questionnaire when he implemented the system, stating the privacy profile of its club. If the two profiles concur, the Privacy Coach states 'match'. If the club gathers more personal data than the customer is willing to give, he is warned 'no match' and he can inquire what the owner actually does with his data.

DIFR developed a test model of the Privacy Coach and demonstrated it at several conferences. Not to sell it as a product, but rather to demonstrate that privacy and empowerment can go hand in hand. Providers of information or products don't have to state their illegible and extensive user agreements, while users can be at ease by just waving their phone.

Scan for a demo of the Privacy Coach.

0011 .0100 Conclusions

Applying RFID to mobile phones opens up many opportunities for innovative services: access, payments and information retrieval on the go. It turns your mobile into a mouse to click on icons in digitalised public space. In a national market dominated by a single player, adoption can go fast while Identity Management issues can be addressed to a single party, as with FeliCa Networks in Japan. In a more global and open constellation, as with NFC, innovation proceeds less smoothly and many Identity Management issues arise. A Trusted Service Manager may therefore be needed to mediate between competitors, transfer data from one provider to another and serve as a single point for applying data legislation and serving customers who like to switch providers.

NFC may yield privacy issues, as more personal data on spending, location and behaviour is registered by more parties. In order to minimise information asymmetries and prevent improper use of user profiles, it is highly recommended that the TSM keeps databases for different functions of NFC services separate from the databases that store personal data. Also, as data retention regulations will apply, it is yet unclear how NFC transactions will need to be retained and what kind of burden this will place on potential service providers. Here too, the TSM can be the single point to enforce these laws and judge whether the costs of data retention are in balance with its benefits.

NFC also offers many opportunities for user empowerment. If given insight into their own transaction histories, users become aware of the digital identities they build up and may even receive some ways to manipulate them. The establishment of a Trusted Service Manager may ensure an open system that is not only accessible to all service providers, but to users too. The TSM can prevent lock-in effects and mediate when a user wants to switch from handset or provider or subscribe to several. Finally, if NFC remains an open system, innovative applications such as the Privacy Coach will get a chance to better serve the needs of users.

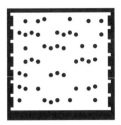

TAG for note 2

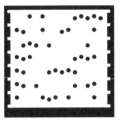

TAG for note 4

TAG for note 5

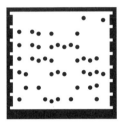

TAG for note 9

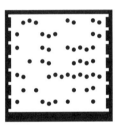

TAG for note 10

Notes

1   Riyako Suketomo, cartes-asia.com www.cartes-asia.com/mobile-FeliCa-5-years-of-mobile-contact-less-business-in-japan accessed on 4 October 2010.

2   W. Hernandez, 18 June 2010, Nokia's Smart Phones to Feature NFC Chips In 2011, paymentssource.com. http://www.paymentssource.com/news/nokia-smart-phones-to-feature-nfc-chips-3002165-1.html accessed on 21 October 2010.

3   S. Clarke, 22 June 2010, 'We didn't mean all smart-phones would get NFC', says Nokia, www.nearfield-communicationsworld.com http://www.nearfield-communicationsworld.com/2010/06/22/34001/we-didnt-mean-all-smartphones-would-get-nfc-says-nokia/ Accessed on 20 October 2010.

4   Interview Christian van 't Hof (18 August 2010) with Junyu Wang, associate professor and associate director Auto-ID Lab China. Fudan University, Department of Microelectronics. Shanghai China.

5   Interview Christian van 't Hof (20 August 2010) with Songlin Feng, president of the Shanghai Advanced Research Institute.

6   Anonymous, 5 February 2010, ecommerce Journal http://ecommerce-journal.com/node/26782 accessed on 21 October 2010.

7   D Armstrong, M. Bayings and M.D. Desertine, 2008, interviews.

8   Anonymous, 9 September 2010, Banken en operators gaan vor grootschalige invoering NFC TelecomPaper.com http://www.telecompaper.com/nl/article.aspx?cid=755719, accesed on 4 October 2010.

9   Hof, C. van 't. (2007) 'RFID and Identity Management in Everyday Life' The Hague: Rathenau Institute, in assignment of the European Parliament.

10 Broenink, G. et al 'The Privacy Coach: Supporting customer privacy in the Internet of Things' http://www.autoidlabs.org/events/ciot2010/

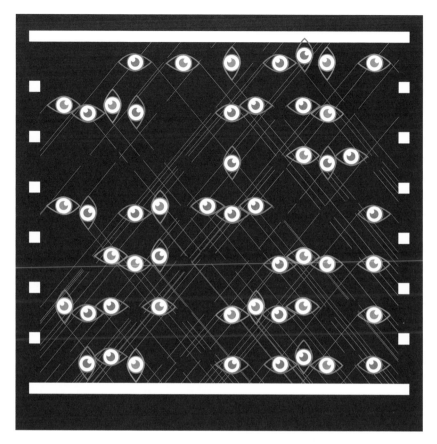

Case 0100

Street Images

Ad Schreijenberg, Christian van 't Hof
and Jolanda Koffijberg

'The boundaries between
public and private are
blurring more and more.'

A Glance Behind the Scenes of Camera Surveillance

Camera surveillance is one of the most familiar examples of the digitalisation of public space, and it is still evolving. Although it is difficult to prove whether Closed Circuit Television (CCTV) actually helps to make the streets safer, both citizens and governments share a wish to expand its use. London is currently one of the most densely surveyed areas, but some Dutch cities, like Rotterdam, come close.

CCTV Identity Management is not only about identifying the persons being watched, it also involves identifying who is watching. In the Netherlands, fierce debates in the 1990s resulted in legislation on who is allowed to watch whom and under what circumstances. Currently, enforcement of the legislation is becoming more and more difficult as both public and private parties increasingly capture and exchange images. Closed Circuit Television is turning in to Shared Circuit Television. This case describes how the regulating watchful eyes are being regulated themselves in an evolving national network.

0100 .0001 Look Who is Watching

Public space in the Netherlands yields more and more cameras. Often a sign is attached that indicates the presence of surveillance and contains a section of the law. Whose cameras are they, how many cameras are there and who is allowed to see us? We make a distinction between public cameras – owned by the municipality, the police etc. – and private cameras – owned by companies and private persons.

[● REC]

The number of public cameras in the Netherlands is known (there are around 3,000), but the number of private cameras in public space is not registered. We know that in Great Britain, around ten per cent of all cameras in public space are owned by the authorities.[1] The total number of cameras in the UK is estimated at 2.5 million.[2] In 2010, there were 10,524 (public and private) cameras in the city of London, thus an estimated number of 1000 public cameras.[3] In comparison: in Rotterdam, the town with the largest number of public cameras in the Netherlands, there are approximately 300 public cameras. With its one million inhabitants, it has a camera density similar to that of London.

In addition, a sample survey showed that in 2008, a quarter of all Dutch retail establishments had CCTV.[4] Moreover, public transport companies also make use of CCTV. And outside the reach of all these cameras you can still be recorded. Citizens use their mobile phones ever more often to record incidents, and the Dutch authorities even launched a campaign to promote this phenomenon.[5]

Is anyone allowed to put up cameras wherever they like, and watch? No, there is a legal framework. After the fierce debates of the 1990s, Dutch municipalities were authorised to apply CCTV in 2004. Rights and obligations are outlined in both the Local Government Act and the Police Data Act. Reports on the effectiveness and efficiency of camera surveillance must be offered to the local council. In the same year, secret CCTV was penalised under Article 441b of the Dutch criminal code.[6] Which specific law applies in what case currently depends on the type of camera surveillance and the objective of CCTV. If the objective is to monitor public order (Local Government Act) or tracing (Code of Criminal Procedure), privacy aspects are regulated by the Police Data Act. If the objective is related to management or the protection of property (Civil Code), the Protection of Personal Data Act applies.

In sum, the police are allowed to watch images of all public spaces and store them for later use, while private parties may primarily watch and act on images of mostly private spaces. This legal framework appears well organised. However, in practice it is less manageable. It turns out that it is hard to prove whether CCTV actually works, while at the same time public and private surveillance are overlapping more and more.

Panopticon

The concept of the Panopticon was originally developed by philosopher Bentham in 1785 as a prison design. Prison cells would be placed in a circular form, with a watch tower in the centre. The guard could see all the prisoners from his viewpoint, while the prisoners could not see whether they were being watched or not.

According to the philosopher Michel Foucault (1926-1984), the presumed constant presence of the watchful eye in the Panopticon would be internalised by the prisoners, leading to socially acceptable behaviour. He claimed this stands as a model for the rest of society as well, as we are continuously being watched. Still, this model would not necessary lead to tyranny, as the centre of the panopticon could be controlled democratically. Who is allowed in the watchtower and watch under which circumstances?[7]

Many surveillance studies refer to the panoptic model. Still one could wonder whether it suits camera surveillance. People may refrain from petty crime once they know they are being watched, but when it comes to violence under influence of alcohol or drugs, they may not. Also, CCTV currently does not really have a centre of control; it rather functions as a network. This makes it impossible to have a total overview, as well as a single point of control.

0100 .0010 CCTV is Perceived as Desirable, but is it Effective?

Both citizens and municipalities regard camera surveillance as an important means to increase safety in the streets. Still, the effectiveness of CCTV raises many questions: the positive effects of camera surveillance have never been indisputably proven.[8] Still, more and more companies, private persons and municipalities use cameras, and once they have been installed, there is not much of a chance that they will be removed. It seems illogical to use a tool of which the effects have not been proven yet. Both citizens and the authorities sometimes tend to have very high expectations of CCTV. However, its costs are very high. The total installation costs of an average CCTV-project are above €300,000 and the management costs are estimated at an additional €70,000 per year.[9]

The effect of CCTV can also be negative if images are used for improper purposes. For example, pictures were made by CCTV in a car park of famous Dutch football player Wesley Sneijder kissing the girlfriend of a popular Dutch singer, which were shown on Dutch television in a tabloid talk show. Such incidents show the risk of camera footage.

Municipalities and the police take care that the private spaces of citizens are not visible on-screen with CCTV by means of so-called masking techniques. In this way, windows are digitally masked.[10] In spite of this, CCTV in public domains inevitably leads to reduced privacy for citizens. That is why 54 per cent of the Dutch municipalities with CCTV consider it important to ask citizens beforehand whether they regard it as desirable.[11] In addition, 57 per cent of the municipalities with CCTV have a complaints procedure for citizens. Moreover, after the implementation, municipalities also conduct evaluations to examine whether a far-reaching measure such as CCTV is permanently necessary.

Although it is not easy to evaluate the effects of camera surveillance, evaluations often lead to the conclusion that CCTV functions well. If, for instance, the police register more incidents, this may indicate that crime has increased and that the cameras should stay. It could also be an indication that with the help of cameras, extra incidents are registered, which also means that the purpose of the installation of cameras is met. Because of this, the decision to remove existing cameras is not easily taken.

The new passport as a biometric data gatherer

In Europe, the US, China, Japan and an increasing number of other countries, passports are equipped with RFID chips that contain biometric information. This can be a portrait, which is digitalised in such a way that 24 unique points on your face work as a unique identifier, or digitalised fingerprints. What if this information could be stored in a database, with which crime suspects could be identified? The Netherlands is unique in the world in its aim for such a database, as it has passed a law that enables the reuse of biometrics from national passports for police investigation.

The biometric passport led to many protests around the world. In the UK for example, activists spread the digitalised fingerprints of the prime minister on the internet. In China, fingerprints are not taken at all, as they claim that 'you only do that to criminals'.[12] Germany already stated at the proposal of the new passport that it will only store data on the chip and not centrally, as this is perceived as a very intrusive state interference. In the end, all countries must adhere to the ICANN standards and use the biometric chip.

Whether or not to store the data is up to the countries themselves.

In 2006, the Dutch Ministry of Internal Affairs developed plans for ORRA: an on-line register for passport data. In the original proposal, this register would serve to combat fraud. Nevertheless, the new passport law, which was passed on 11 June 2009, clearly states that biometric data can also be used for the prosecution of criminal acts and in case the national security of the Netherlands or its allies is at stake. Although it is unprecedented throughout the world, the law was passed with little public debate.

When the first passports were issued in 2007, the Rathenau Institute carried out a national survey among Dutch citizens in order to ask them whether this database should be used for police investigation. Statements on the use of fingerprints or facial scans in order to compare them with CCTV images all received a majority approval. Nevertheless, many experts warn that the biometric database will be a national danger in itself: the system will be hacked and identities will be stolen. Also, using biometrics to identify suspects is risky: there is a chance that two different photos or fingerprints might match. Above all, it is a matter of principle: citizens have no choice as they need a passport. This is a system with no way out, with which we may trust the current government, but what about in the future? After the elections, the parliamentary debate on a centralised, biometric database opened up again on 7 October 2010. Although the law is already there, it's up to the new government to decide whether they will actually build the database.

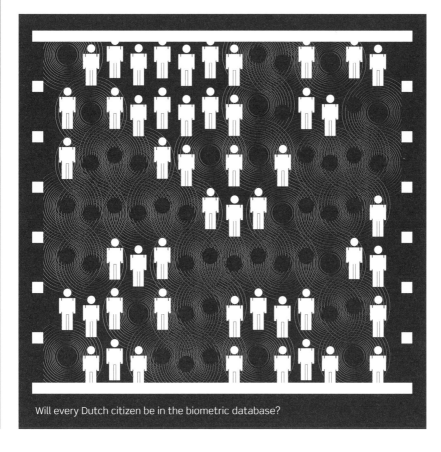

25
.TAG

Will every Dutch citizen be in the biometric database?

0100
.0011 Towards a Smart, National Street Image Network

The technique behind CCTV currently follows two trends: an increase in the sharing of footage and smarter cameras. Camera footage can be exchanged more easily due to standardisation, the regional connection of cameras, and public-private cooperation. It is observed that networks are standardised, so that footage of all cameras can be obtained, transported and stored in the same way. This enables communication between various systems. This technical development enables the connection of local camera projects in regional centres. Recently, a regional surveillance centre has opened in Eindhoven, and Amsterdam also plans to assemble camera footage in a regional surveillance centre.[13] The different CCTV systems (public and private) now seem to evolve into one network.

Within this network, public and private parties increasingly share footage. Business parks and shopping centres are secured with cameras installed at the initiative of both private and public partners. Not only the premises of the shop or company are filmed, but also a part of the public space, in order to also bring into vision access roads to these companies. Due to such practices, the boundaries between public and private are blurring more and more:

1   Public camera footage can be viewed by private parties, under supervision of a police officer.
2   The police are using camera footage that originated from private cameras.
3   Citizens actively disseminate homemade footage of incidents, both from criminals and misbehaving police officers, on the internet.

In the Netherlands, citizens are encouraged to film incidents with their own cameras, and the British company Internet Eyes takes it yet another step further. The company is going to disseminate camera footage of shops and public spaces. People who are interested can watch this footage and earn 1,000 pounds if they catch a thief and report this by means of sending a text message to the shopkeeper. According to the company, British citizens know that footage produced by the large quantity of cameras in their country is not viewed real-time, which reduces the chance of arresting the perpetrator. Shopkeepers now take security matters in their own hands.[14]

The second trend that can be observed is the development of new techniques that provide cameras with more options than simply the recording of footage. These cameras are called 'smart cameras'. Some camera systems are able to detect motion. Such systems are used in places where no movement should occur, for instance, such as stations which are locked up at night or harbour areas. When the system detects movement, the operator in the CCTV centre receives a signal. Footage analysis is even more advanced: movement is not only detected, but the footage is also interpreted. Number plate recognition, which is used during motorway controls, for instance, is one of the applications of footage analysis which already functions fairly reliably.[15] A specific type of footage analysis is face recognition. In public transport in Rotterdam, face recognition technology is used in the enforcement of public transport bans. If a public transport ban has been imposed on you, your photograph is taken and subsequently stored in a database. A smart camera at the entrance of the metro provides a signal when it recognises a person who matches one of the photographs in the database. This way, it is possible to enforce the public transport ban.[16]

0100 .0100 Conclusions

Being one of the oldest applications in the digitalisation of public places, CCTV provides us with examples on how identities are managed on the streets. Dutch legislation from the 1990s clearly distinguishes between private and public supervisors where it concerns their competences. Police are allowed to watch images of all public spaces and store them for later use, while private parties primarily have to watch and act on images of mostly private spaces. Because an increasing number of parties collect and exchange footage, this distinction becomes more difficult to maintain. The situation cannot be described as a panopticon – after all, there is no apparent centre – but it tends towards a surveillance network in which anyone can watch anyone, in principle. This situation can become problematic if footage is used illegitimately. Moreover, current legislation does not prescribe evaluation: what are the actual costs of camera surveillance and does it provide the desired results?

Therefore, it is important to review in what way we want to regulate regulating footage. It should be clear to the people in the streets who is allowed to watch and be watched and under what circumstances. Anonymity should therefore be the default setting in public places, but if security is at stake, this anonymity will be lifted. Smart cameras, which only send in footage if something actually happens, could be helpful in this regard. Face recognition can be used to identify suspects, but the same applies to this technology: it should be clear who is allowed to use it and under what circumstances.

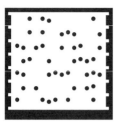

TAG for note 1

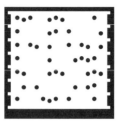

TAG for note 2

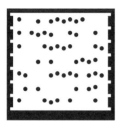

TAG for note 5

TAG for note 10

TAG for note 14

Notes

1 C. Norris, M. McCahill and D. Wood (2004). Editiorial. The Growth of CCTV: a global perspective on the international diffusion of video surveillance in publicly accessible space. The Politics of CCTV in Europe and Beyond.(http://www.surveillance-and-society.org/cctv.htm).

2 Public Attitudes to the Deployment of Surveillance Techniques (2004). Sharpe Research Ltd. (http://www.ico.gov.uk/upload/documents/library/corporate/research_and_reports/public_attitudes_research.pdf).

3 London Evening Standard, 27 August 2010. *Tens of thousands of CCTV cameras, yet 80% of crime unsolved.* (http://www.thisislondon.co.uk/news/article-23412867-tens-of-thousands-of-cctv-cameras-yet-80-of-crime-unsolved.do).

4 WODC (2009). *Monitor criminaliteit en bedrijfsleven.* Feiten en trends inzake aard en omvang van criminaliteit in het bedrijfsleven. The Hague: WODC. (http://www.rijksoverheid.nl/bestanden/documenten-en-publicaties/rapporten/2009/06/23/monitor-criminaliteit-bedrijfsleven-2008/monitorcriminaliteitbedrijfsleven2008.pdf)

5 http://www.nederlandveilig.nl/veiligheidopstraat/tips/#tip4

6 Smeets, A. (2004). *Camera's in het publieke domein.* Privacynormen voor het cameratoezicht op de openbare orde. The Hague: College Bescherming Persoonsgegevens.

7 Foucault, M. (1989). Discipline, toezicht en straf. Groningen: Historische Uitgeverij.

8 Schreijenberg, A., Koffijberg, J en Dekkers, S. (2009) *Cameratoezicht in de openbare ruimte, driemeting.* Amsterdam: Regioplan. On the basis of national and international studies, the Netherlands Institute for Social Research (SCP) also draws the conclusion that the effectiveness of formal surveillance by means of cameras still raises many questions. Noije, L. en Wittebrood, K. (2009) *Overlast en verloedering ontsleuteld.* Veronderstelde en werkelijke effecten van het Actieplan overlast en verloedering. The Hague: SCP.

9 Schreijenberg, A., Koffijberg, J en Dekkers, S. (2009) *Cameratoezicht in de openbare ruimte, driemeting.* Amsterdam: Regioplan, p. 29.

10 http://epcomsecurity.com/images/privacy_masking.jpg

11 Schreijenberg, A., Koffijberg, J en Dekkers, S. (2009) *Cameratoezicht in de openbare ruimte, driemeting.* Amsterdam: Regioplan.

12 Interview Christian van 't Hof (20 August 2010) with Songlin Feng, president of the Shanghai Advanced Research Institute.

13 http://www.hetccv.nl/instrumenten/Cameratoezicht+publiek+privaat/RPC+Oost+Brabant+en+RPC+IJsselland+-+Het+RTR%AEconcept

14 http://interneteyes.co.uk/

15 http://en.wikipedia.org/wiki/Automatic_number_plate_recognition

16 http://nos.nl/artikel/160201-camera-ov-rotterdam-herkent-gezichten.html and http://www.nuvideo.nl/algemeen/40299/gezichtsherkenning-in-ov-rotterdam-bijna-zover.html

Case 0101

Geoweb

Christian van 't Hof, Floortje Daemen
and Rinie van Est

'A tension grows between
what we want to see and
what we want to show
of ourselves.'

All Information on Earth

This chapter is about geo-data: digital information plotted on maps. We first describe how Google enables us to zoom in on the earth: from satellite pictures, to aerial photography, to street view. We then show that this digital mirror image of the earth presents a commercial and social platform to augment information and images on specific places. The next phase in this development comes when the data plotted on the map is shown live. Geo-data opens up many new opportunities for services, but also new threats. How can we manage our identity in these interwoven worlds? In what ways do these digital maps empower us as we move through public space and in what ways do they infringe upon our privacy? This case shows that as the physical and virtual worlds become increasingly interwoven, a tension grows between what we want to see and what we want to show of ourselves.

0101 .0001 How Google Democratised and Commercialised Geo-Data

Until recently, detailed geographic pictures taken from high up in the sky were a matter of national security. The first images date back from the beginning of the 20th century and were used for military purposes and issues on landownership.[1] Aerial imagery gained momentum during the Second World War and again in its aftermath during the Cold War.[2] In the beginning of the 1960s, military observation satellites Explorer and Discoverer provided the first satellite images to the US government. These images weren't live, as films were launched physically from the satellites and needed to be tracked, found and developed later on. The first live imagery was provided in 1976 by the Keyhole satellite, part of the Landsat programme which still runs today.[3] Aside from military purposes, the images were increasingly put to civil use: meteorological observation, land planning and environmental management. In the mean-time, countries increasingly collaborated and together they created a full virtual image of the Earth.[4]

Satellite imagery was first commercialised in 2000 by the Californian company Keyhole Inc. They applied gaming technology to the imagery and developed Earth Viewer. This software application fused the pictures in such a way it gave a smooth scrolling experience, flying through the sky and diving in on specific places. It also allowed for plotting information on specific locations of the maps such as addresses, phone numbers and business information. Keyhole's business model was based on subscriptions to the service. This did not turn out to be very profitable. Still, Keyhole gained popularity, especially in 2003, when CNN used their maps for broad-casting the US bombing of Baghdad.[5]

Since then, many big companies rushed in to launce their own geo-data platforms: Mapquest, Yahoo! Local Maps and Microsoft Bing Maps. In 2005 Google bought Keyhole Inc., renamed the application Google Earth and offered it for free to internet users. Google 's business model is very different from that of Keyhole: they aim to make all information on earth available to everyone and gain revenues from advertisements people see and click on while they search through this information.[6] The virtual images of the Earth thereby became more than just a map; it has become a platform for advertisements.

The Google Earth platform consists of the fusion of real footage and an innumerable set of virtual layers projected on it. At the highest altitude level there are the satellite images, provided by the US company Digital Globe. Their satellites Quickbird and Worldview 1 and 2 orbit the earth and photograph about one million square metres of the earth a day. The more important an area is (e.g. a city), the higher the resolution. The satellites send their photos to stations in Alaska and Norway, which transfer them to a data centre in Colorado. There the data is supplemented with aerial images taken by planes, converted into 3D models and smoothened to create a seamless zoom-in experience. Essential to the synthesis of all this data are the GPS coordinates: they form the grid onto which all images can be placed and scaled on the right spot. The GPS coordinates are also the basis for the layer of the Street View photos and location information.

Street level views are gathered by the Google cars, which have nine multi-directional cameras placed on top, providing an image 360 degrees around and 270 degrees vertically. GPS systems inside the cars determine where the images should be placed on Google Earth and Maps.[7] The first street images were gathered in 2007 in big cities in US, and they gradually expanded to include European cities, Japan and the rest of the world.

On top of this photographic image of the whole Earth and its GPS grid underneath, all sorts of virtual layers can be added: roadmaps, contact information, 3D images of buildings, events, and so on. People can also upload photos of specific locations. Moreover, the platform is increasingly used by organisations that project live data onto it. Google has therefore succeeded in developing a single platform for projecting all the information on Earth.

0101 Identity Management
.0010 Within a Digitalised Image
of the Earth

The empowerment provided by the Google Earth platform is evident. Users gather information in order to find their way, orientate on destinations, scan the environment and search for anything that might meet their interests. It also provides them a new way of sending out information by

27
.TAG

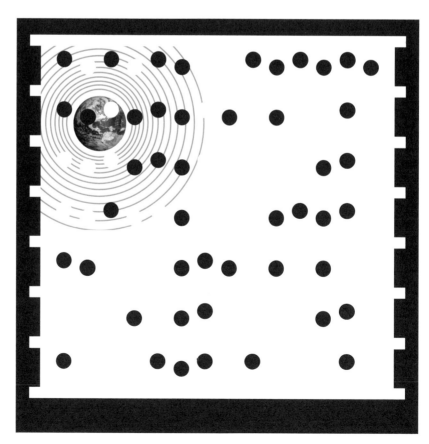

placing it on the map. Communication is complemented with coordinates. But what about privacy? When does the Google Earth Platform show things we don't want others to see? Who is in control of this data? And what can we do about it?

The first issues start at a latitude of several hundred metres, where one can distinguish buildings and private property. When Google launched Google Earth in the Netherlands in 2005, there was a parliamentary debate on the question whether the images would be a danger to national security, as terrorists might use the map to find sensitive targets. Minister Donner of Justice claimed there was no danger, as Google uses images that are already publicly available. Moreover, the people who provide these images adhere to the law on aerial photography.[8] This law, dating back from 1959, states that one is not allowed to take pictures of military objects and royal estates. A list of these objects is compiled by the Dutch Military Intelligence and Security Service. Therefore, these objects are not visible on Google Earth and replaced by typical green and gray triangles. Still, one could wonder whether this typical way of concealing sensitive objects would rather make it easier for terrorists to spot a target.

Aerial imagery also led to concerns among citizens, as private property, like gardens which were previously hidden behind fences, could now be spotted from above. In Great Britain this led to so-called pool crashing. Youngsters would scan Google Earth for private pools and arrange a massive invasion, organised through social media. Returning pool owners would find their gardens littered with empty beer cans and other trash.[9] Google's position on phenomena like these is that the aerial imagery they use is already publicly available and they don't show anything else than images one could already retrieve through other means. The only thing they do is make it easier to search through these images.[10] Still, Google does change our perspective by doing so. Exemplary is the case of a Belgium fountain in Maasmechelen. Viewed from above, the fountain formed a swastika – the symbol of Nazi Germany. Citizens scrolling over the map of their town showed concerns and the local government reconstructed the object to make it less offensive.[11]

Once Google started using their Google cars to collect street level views, up to the point that one can distinguish persons, vehicles and houses, the debate became more serious. The ways in which different countries govern street photography differs strongly. In the US, the law allows that you are photographed as you move through public places, since it is considered 'public'. In contrast, the Dutch Data Protection Act defines a picture of a person's face as personal data.[12] Although laws governing street images vary across countries, public response to Street View showed many similarities.

When Street View was launched in 2008 in the US, there was a public outcry from people who saw this application as a huge infringement on their privacy, because they would lose anonymity in public places. Google responded to these concerns by implementing their 'face blurring technology'.[13] Also, a button was added to the interface where one could

The Dutch Ministry of Defence appears to need privacy.

report inappropriate images and file a request to remove them. These measures were also implemented in other countries, but this did not take away all public concerns. In Japan it turned out the Street View cars did not only record the street images but also peered into private properties through windows or over fences.[14] Google therefore had to adjust the height of

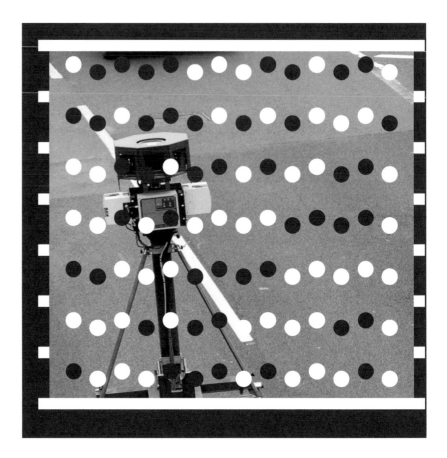

the cameras. Citizens of the British village Broughton even blocked Google cars form entering their streets, which are therefore still not visible on-line.[15] Germany took an even firmer stand, claiming Google should not only anonymise data while publishing, but they should also store it anonymously. The Czech Republic took it a step further and even banned the Google Street View cars from its streets altogether.[16]

In the Netherlands, Street View did not trigger much controversy. When it was launched in March 2009, some national celebrities were actually recognised while standing on their doorsteps, even though there faces were blurred. They claimed this would disclose their residential address and requested Google to remove the images. On the other hand, some people responded with great enthusiasm, and began searching for images of people in uncompromising positions, linking to them from popular weblogs such as streetview.nl and GeenStijl.nl ('no style'). The collections of images contain men entering sex shops, police officers committing offences, women in sexy dresses and men peeing by the side of the road.

The biggest controversy concerning Street View until now arose when it turned out that the Google cars were not just collecting images but also scooped Wi-Fi signals coming from people's homes. In doing so, they could potentially eavesdrop on the communication of unprotected networks. In the US, Consumer Watchdog President Jamie Court called Google's actions 'the most massive example of wire-tapping in American history.' Similar concerns were raised in Australia, Spain, Great Britain and Germany. Google spokespeople responded by claiming the code was collected accidentally; they apologised and stated the error would be corrected.[17]

These examples demonstrate the two sides of the company's philosophy: 'To make all information on Earth available'. On the one hand, it is empowering to users to get more information. On the other hand, not everybody wants everybody to know about their whereabouts. It appears that Google simply gathers and disseminates up to the point that someone starts protesting. Being seen appears to be the default setting, anonymity an opt-out.

0101 .0011 Toward Real-Time Maps

Google, along with many other companies and governments, have digitalised almost every location on earth. Accordingly, physical space is supplemented by virtual space and augmented with location specific information. Public space is now in the net. The next step in geo-data is adding the time factor: it is not only relevant where the data was gathered, but also when it was gathered. There is a clear trend towards real-time location data. Already some applications are being built based on this notion.

In most cases, the key technology for live maps is the mobile phone, both for tracking people as well as displaying data to them. Using the strength of the signals that the phone receives from the nearest antennas, its location can be calculated up until a few metres. Tracking phones has been obligatory for security reasons in the US and Europe since the beginning of the millennium. If a person calls an emergency number, the mobile network operators automatically log the location of the phone, not only to direct the emergency services but also to prevent people from abusing the number. Additional laws were implemented in 2005 and 2006, resulting in the so-called data retention directives (see first chapter), requiring mobile network operators (MNOs) to store who made a call and with whom, were and when.

Companies can use this data too, as long as they comply with the data protection directives. The case study on networked cars demonstrated this. MNO Vodafone tracks signals from mobile phones in cars in order to measure the amount and the speed of traffic. As this is all the data they need, every signal is given a random number each hour, resulting in a live map of moving dots. The data is used by TomTom to inform drivers about traffic jams and by RDW for traffic management. A total overview of all live traffic in the Netherlands is expected by 2015. By then, there should also be a live map of all public transport, based on GPS signals of vehicles and numbers of people who checked in with their public transport card. These systems are allowed to track people and display the numbers on a map, as they are nothing more than that: anonymous numbers.

Phone signals for counting people are also used in academic research, for example by Current City, a collaboration of several universities doing research on crowd behaviour. This research foundation draws vivid maps of cities like Rome and Amsterdam, plotting the number of people in the streets with yellow bars that change through time. Phone signals are anonymised, aggregated and analysed, by which they can claim that 'without impinging on the privacy of individual network subscribers, our analyses provide important information on the concentration and relative weights of human activities within a given urban environment.'[18] Practical applications involve crowd control, traffic management and urban planning.

When mobile phones are not just used for tracking and counting people, but also for providing information back to them, anonymity does not seem to be an option. Companies provide their services for free, but they need to customise it to your behaviour and find you to send advertisements. Here again, we see Google as one of the frontrunners. Google Latitude is a mobile application for finding friends and family, based on either the GSM signal of your mobile phone or the IP address of their personal computer. Users send their location data to their selection of other users by pushing a button. Their location is plotted on Google Maps along with a time stamp. Naturally, your account is integrated into all services Google provides and used to customise marketing. Other services, such as FriendFinder or IYOUIT work according to the same principle, but they don't have the powerful Google grid to integrate all services and profit from targeted advertorials.

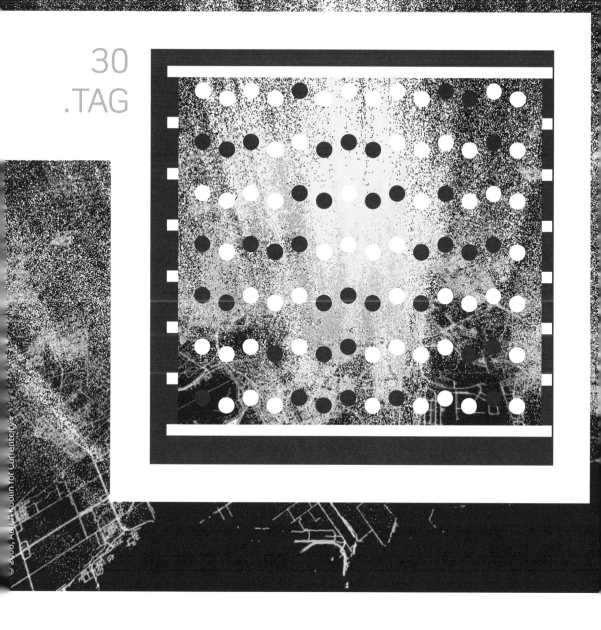

With the increased use of smart phones, enabled with much more computer power and GPS localisation, the location-based services became even faster and more accurate. Take as an example m.google.com, which provides a local search for smart phones. Type in 'coffee' and you'll see the nearest coffee bar, again plotted on Google Maps. Or take Foursquare, which activates social networks based on location. Just like the other friend finding tools, contacts (retrieved from your address book, Twitter account or Facebook) are located and share their opinion on these locations. But they are also involved in a popularity game. If you 'check in' to a location, you gather points for it. The person who checked in most becomes the major and is displayed on the site.

As these services are all personalised, users need to be informed about the fact that their location data is being used. Foursquare, Google Latitude and the likes, all show a pop-up on your phone, asking whether your location can be used. Although this may appear as a clear choice, it remains unclear what actually happens with the data. Most user licence agreements (which you probably haven't read but did formally agree upon by ticking a box) are extensive, illegible texts full of references to websites. In principle, these companies can do anything with your data, while still complying with data protection directives. To make things even more complicated, these service providers increasingly collaborate, exchanging personal data from different applications, leaving users confused about who is actually managing their identity.

Children Security Services in Japan

Live maps can also be built on other technologies, such as RFID. In Japan, the Kodomo Mimamori, or 'child security' service, is an interesting example. Children carry a tag with them which is read by one of the readers placed on the power lines. Areas where kids play and go to school are covered by placing one reader at every 200 metres. When the kids go to school, their live signal is plotted on a map, which can be viewed by parents on their mobile phones or pc at home. They can also subscribe to an SMS service and receive a message when their child passes a certain station, for example, the entry of the school. The first successful implementation was in 2007 in Warabi, where 800 of 1500 children carried the tag. Interestingly, both the children and parents did not see privacy issues. Moreover, the kids exchanged their log-in codes in order to track each other.[19] During our last visit in 2009, 14 municipalities had already joined the programme.[20]

0101 .0100 Conclusions

Google changed the way we perceive our Earth by broadening our perspective: the whole earth, seen from a distance of many kilometres up until a few metres from the ground. This provides users with great opportunities for empowerment: not only to watch what is going on elsewhere, but moreover to publish data according to specific locations. The time factor plays an increasingly important role in geo-data: when was the data gathered; is it live? In order to achieve the scenario of a real-time map, data should be gathered and marked according to time and space variables. Businesses seem to take advantage of this opportunity, while governments appear to lag behind. There is an opportunity for governments to improve their services: they could make information that is relevant to citizens available to them by placing it on the map.

At the same time, we don't want everyone to see everything about everybody. Laws on aerial photography may turn out to be outdated once the blurred spots are perceived to not actually conceal sensitive spots, but rather directly point at them. Going down to street level, it appears that Google first gathers and publishes as much as possible, and then they see whether it is appropriate or not by providing an opt-out. Providers for location-based services appear to take the same approach and see themselves legally protected by illegible User Licence Agreements that no user actually reads. The only counterforce seems to be public opinion, but for most people it is unclear what happens to their location data and who is actually using it.

More transparency towards users is needed, but this may not be sufficient. Therefore, data protection rules should be specified to the geographical dimensions. The data minimisation principle for public places could be: *anonymity is the default setting*. This implies that the location of users is only published once they clearly choose to do so. Even better would be a clear option on *who* would be able to see your location. This minimisation principle will not only protect people's privacy, it will also help to develop new services. Once data on a moving mobile is anonymous, businesses, governments, researchers and other users may gain from information plotted on a live map. This is where privacy and empowerment really go hand in hand.

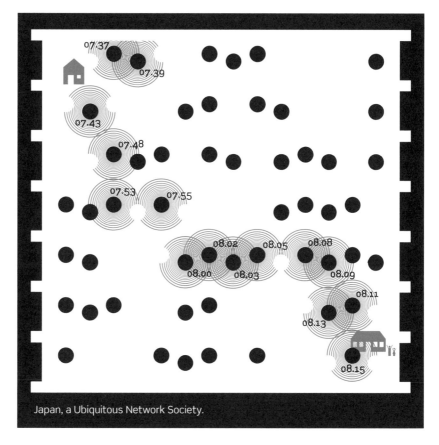

Japan, a Ubiquitous Network Society.

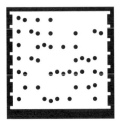

TAG for note 5

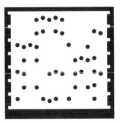

TAG for note 10

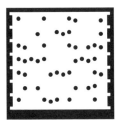

TAG for note 15

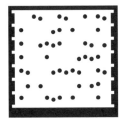

TAG for note 18

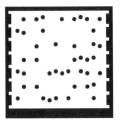

TAG for note 19

Notes

1   Morain, S.A. (1998). 'A brief history of remote sensing applications, with emphasis on Landsat'. In: Liverman, D.M. et al. (eds.) People and Pixels: Linking Remote Sensing and Social Science. Washington-DC: National Research Council, pp. 28–50.

2   Campbell, J.B. (2002). Introduction to remote sensing. (3rd edition) London: Taylor & Francis.

3   Idem Morain, S.A. (1998).

4   Idem Campbell, J.B. (2002).

5   Stross, R. (2008). 'Planet Google. One Company's Audacious Plan to Organize Everything We Know.' New York: First Free Press; The Economist (2007). 'The world on your desktop'. In: The Economist, 6 September 2007.

6   Idem Stross, R. (2008).

7   Google (2009). 'Maps Nederland. Achter de schermen.' Source: http://www.google.nl/help/maps/streetview/behind-the-scenes.html (visited 4 October 2010).

8   Tweede Kamer (2005), 'Vergaderjaar 2005–2006, aanhangsel. KVR24034, 2040519720, 0506tkkvr111.' The Hague: Sdu Uitgevers.

9   Salkeld, L. (2008). 'The Google Earth gatecrashers who take uninvited dips in home-owners' swimming pools.' Mail Online News (visited 30 June).

10 According to Google's Privacy Center at Google: http://www.google.com/intl/nl/privacy_faq.html#toc-earth-images (visited 24 November 2009).

11 Nu.nl (26 July 2006). 'Internetters ontdekken hakenkruis-fontein via Google Earth.' http://www.nu.nl/internet/788492/internetters-ontdekken-hakenkruis-fontein-via-google-earth.html (visited 26 June 2008).

12 Arnbak, A. (2008) 'Zoom in op het Rokin? Google Street View versus het recht op privacy in Nederland' University of Amsterdam.

13 Zhu, Jianjun (2008). 'Street View turns 1, keeps on growing.' Source: http://google-latlong.blogspot.com/2008/06/street-view-turns-1-keeps-on-growing.html (visited 10 June 2008).

14 BBC News (2008). 'Street View under fire in Japan.' Source: http://news.bbc.co.uk/2/hi/technology/8049490.stm (visited 9 December 2009).

15 Schroeder, S. (4 March 2009). 'Google Street View car blocked in UK town.' Source: Mashable.com (visited 4 October 2010).

16 Clint Boulton (2010) 'Google Street View Banned in Czech Republic' In: eWeek.com, (visited 22 September 2010).

17 Brian Prince (2010) 'Google Steet View Privacy Controversy Touches Congress' In: eWeek.com (visited 9 July 2010).

18 http://www.currentcity.org (visited 4 October 2010).

19 Schilpzand, W. & Hof, C. van 't (2008). 'RFID as the Key to the Ubiquitous Network Society. A Japanese Case Study on Identity Management.' Den Haag: Rathenau Institute, TU Eindhoven and the Royal Dutch Embassy in Japan.

20 Interview Christian van 't Hof (3 July 2009) with Ishima en Sanao Orri, Ministry of Internal Affairs and Communication, Tokyo.

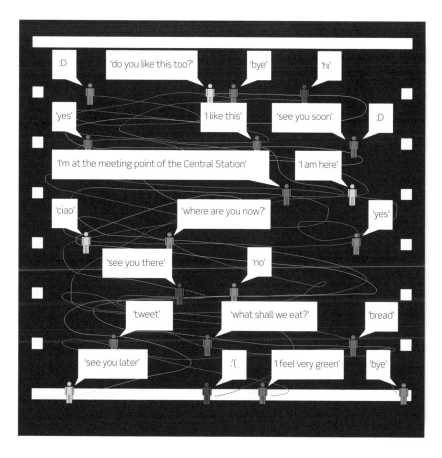

Case 0110

Living Maps

Christian van 't Hof and Floortje Daemen

'Big Brother, once a warning against totalitarianism, now has become a symbol of the importance of being known.'

Designing the Future

This case study is about a thought experiment. What if all live data coming from smart cards, mobiles, navigation devices, cameras and the like, would be plotted on a digital, geographical platform? What if Google Earth would be live? What kinds of applications could this bring forth? How could these applications empower people? What kinds of privacy problems would occur? How would people manage their virtual identity on this living map?

The Rathenau Institute conducted a series of interactive design sessions in 2009 and 2010 with various groups of people, in order to answer these questions. Our methodology aimed at gathering technological options and public opinions, as well as raising awareness. The sessions also provided insights into what different groups in society think of the digitalisation of public space, and what kinds of questions they raise.

The outcomes of the design sessions teach us that people find the scenario of a living map plausible, or even inevitable. They also see the necessity of profiling in order to get the right information, but they perceive it as problematic as well. In a sense, they grasped the notion of Identity Management. Still, privacy was not their main concern; rather, they fear the tools will make life a bit too predictable and well-managed. Empowerment seems to have its limits too.

0110 .0001 The Scenario of a Living Map

In the preceding case studies we described a variety of devices that connect identities to time and space. If you check in to public transport with a smart card, digits are exchanged between the smart card and a reader, which connect the identity of the card to the unique number of that location. Although these access control systems also put a time stamp on the interaction, it does not provide a live image, as data is buffered and not exchanged immediately. This counts for all sorts of RFID applications: tags are only tracked at the point where they are read and data is generally exchanged with delay. Exchange rates as well as the reading distance may be increased over time, but RFID is a difficult technology for live tracking.

On the other hand, public transport vehicles can be tracked live by using GPS coordinates, which can be exchanged through the mobile phone network. This also holds for road traffic and mobile phones, as we have seen in the previous case studies. These devices enable us to gather data from public space on who or what is currently moving through it. Finally, the streets are increasingly covered by digital CCTV cameras. Images are sometimes viewed afterwards, but can, in principle, be viewed live. All these devices together deliver a sufficient amount of data to generate a living map – at least, it is possible technically.

What the organisational and legal possibilities are is a different issue. Different organisations gather data in their own formats for different purposes and may not be willing or able to share this data at all. Legally, there are all sorts of restrictions on sharing personal data. Nonetheless, the case studies also demonstrate that data is shared increasingly and many organisations push the legal possibilities. We therefore presented partici-pants with the premise: imagine that it is technologically possible and legally acceptable to draw a living map. What would you want to do with it?

0110 .0010 Design Sessions to Gather Opinions and Raise Awareness

The methodology for design sessions was developed by the Rathenau Institute. It draws on our experiences with qualitative research methods such as focus groups, role playing games and scenario gaming. Groups don't need to aim at a consensus, but rather play out their arguments and disa-greements. In contrast to surveys, these qualitative methods are aimed at gathering possible opinions and arguments. Nonetheless, if a particular argumentation is followed throughout different settings by different kinds of participants, it provides some indication of public opinion in general. Also, certain arguments may be confronted by recurring counterarguments, which tells us something about what people believe is actually at stake.

From October 2008 to August 2010 we held 11 design sessions, involving 146 participants. In order to get a broad spectrum of perspectives and arguments, we varied the kinds of participants, the roles they played,

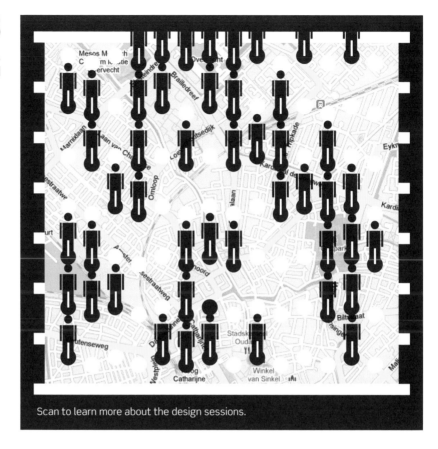

Scan to learn more about the design sessions.

settings[1] they were in, group size, time frame and moderators.[2] Four groups consisted of randomly selected citizens, five group sessions were conducted with experts at conference settings and three sessions were organised at various ministries with civil servants. These sessions ranged from one to three hours, involving 12 to 24 participants. Participants were divided in subgroups of three or four members each, resulting in a total of 35 subgroups and an equal number of applications. Subgroups were assigned different roles based on the organisations they would hypothetically be part of: a ministry, consumer organisation, large telecom business, high tech start-up company, municipality or the like. Participants who did not agree upon their role could switch, or would be appointed a subversive role to sabotage the system of living maps.

Each session followed a similar trajectory. Participants first got a 'technology map': a Google Earth image of the place we were at, devices being placed in there (card readers, navigation devices, cameras, etc.) and a brief explanation on how the technologies work. Then the group was divided in three or four subgroups, with one member being assigned the role of spokesperson. Using large pieces of paper and different coloured pens, they then listed features of their applications and drew possible interfaces and schedules of data flows. Upon the completion of the designs (for an average of one hour), each spokesperson gave a presentation in order to 'sell' their application, while the rest of the group discussed it. All sessions ended with a plenary discussion on living maps in general: the likeliness, appropriateness and possible advantages or problems with it.

0110 .0011 Many Mapping Apps

The design sessions resulted in a total of thirty-five envisioned applications. Some subgroups presented a particular application, for a specific purpose, while other groups came up with a broader concept supported by a whole range of different technologies. At the time we started organising the design sessions, participants took cameras and tags as their prime technology in the net, while at the end of the series the mobile phone proved to be the most popular. This has to do with the increasing popularity of smart phones. Still, current applications of real living maps, such such as Foursquare, as well as the concept of *apps*, were yet unknown to them. Groups had a lot of discussion on who is going to supply the data and who is going to pay for it: businesses, governments or the users themselves. Although some participants were tempted to put too much data on the map at the risk of overwhelming the user, none of the groups failed to come up with a design. Here we categorise the various application designs as networked markets, navigators, preference guides, public security tools and counter maps. Each type of application led to different Identity Management concerns. The concluding section summarises the general patterns in the social discussions about these application types.

0110 .0011 .0001 Networked markets: digitalising demand and supply

Subgroups that took the role of a consumer organisation generally focussed on shopping. The living map would support purchases in supermarkets by offering search options on products and pointing out shops nearby, their prices and reviews. One group also added tags to products, which could be scanned for information on the origins of the products, whether antibiotics were used in the production process or CO_2 emission. The biggest problem was determining who was able to provide the best information: the shops themselves, a consumer authority or other customers. Another problem was the interface. A mobile phone might seem the logical first choice, but it may easily fill up with spam. A small screen on a shopping cart could be another option, but then only the shop owner would be the data supplier, and customers would miss out on information from other sources.

Other subgroups, especially those that took the role of an IT company, worked on both the demand and the supply side. Bringing local producers and local needs together, they offer a platform as well as the mediation and payment. Urban gardening was mentioned as a trend by the company *Big Tree*: vegetables and fruits can be grown and purchased locally once the system brings the two together. Questions were raised on whether this would be more efficient: the products need to travel less, but transport is more expensive with low volumes. Also, small mistakes can have big consequences: for example, 1,000 kg of tomatoes may land on your doorstep instead of the 1,000 grams your thought you ordered.

Finally, a very peculiar application for bringing together supply and demand is *Rent a Cam*. The map shows where someone is filming. If you think it is interesting, you click on it and pay per minute, while the person filming earns a percentage of the revenues. If many people start watching, it may be an indication that something important is happening there, and more people may rush in to start filming too and sell their footage. This could evolve into a very dynamic market for live images.

0110 .0011 .0010 Preference guides: tell me what to do and whom to meet

The leisure sector was also well-represented among the subgroups. Based on profiles, which involve stated preferences, previous visits and a geographical radiance, users are advised about things to do or people nearby. These applications generally also involve all sorts of review options, so people with similar profiles or experiences can inform each other.

For example, *Here & Now* was designed by a cultural institute to inform you on cultural activities nearby. Applications for going out also involved dating applications, which you can use to meet people with similar preferences based on what you would like to do and your relationship status. Some suggested a clear opt-out button for instantly becoming invisible on the map and a function to warn you as soon as an ex-partner is around. Other preference guides focussed on more specific target audiences. For example, think visitors of a conference – *LinkedIn live* – where participants are matched on professionalism and proximity. Or playing football: the map shows football fields through webcams. If the game appeals to you, you can go there and join the team as player or viewer. As this will stimulate amateur sports, there may even be government funding for it.

The difficulty with these applications is the extent to which profiles are personalised. As a user, you want your device to know as much as possible about you in order to specify your preferences. Some of these preferences you want to show to others in order to meet them, but you don't want everybody to know everything about you. Moreover, who is going to manage this profile if you bring together different applications and providers into one device? Companies were perceived as too untrustworthy, so most opted for a non-profit institute, ministry or municipality. Still, anonymous data are useful too. Dots placed on the map function as a crowd radar: which public areas are busy? You may want to go to a busy pub, or you may prefer to go to a spacious area where there are only a few people. The preference guide tells you where to go.

0110 .0011 .0011 Public security tools: total information awareness

As many subgroups took the role of the Ministry of Justice or the police, we received many security applications labelled as a variation of *Big Brother*. Some took the concept of a living map quite literally: law enforcement can use Google Earth, where it seamlessly zooms in on street level through live cameras. Individual criminals can be spotted and identified. In line with the concept of panopticon, the continuous presence of a watchful eye may have a disciplinary effect, preventing people to misbehave. The security map can also be used for military purposes or disaster management: allocating resources and crowd control. Augmenting specific data on people moving on the map provide additional security options, for example in the case of maps plotted with data on the official emergency services available or citizens who have First Aid capabilities. One subgroup proposed tracking young children for their security. Another popular application is tagging convicts. During or after their punishment, they can move freely on the streets, while a watchful eye checks whether they don't fall back into old habits or go near their victims.

At ground level, applications may support police officers during their work on the street. Some envisioned cyber cops with goggles that recognise people, combine ID with information and scan for dangerous behaviour. This device automatically scans an officer's iris for identification to determine whether he is allowed access to this sensitive information and appropriate information to his function (traffic officer, crime investigation). Citizens, too, may be involved in making the streets safer by filming crime and sending it with GPS coordinates to the police. In this way, they can overcome their innocent bystander dilemma. Still, they may also use the system to film the performance of the officer involved in solving the crime.

The general response to applications like these is that security outweighs privacy as long as the stakes are high. Different access levels based on authorisation are pleaded for. In case of serious crime, the highest authorities have access to all data, lower authorities dealing with petty crime see less. Citizens' involvement in solving street crime is seen as a logical next step, but it should be handled with care, as they are not trained to do police work and they are expected to be biased in their judgements. For police officers, these public security tools may empower them with location-based and live information, but it may also give them a feeling of losing control, as this system may outsmart human police work or be used by supervisors and citizens for monitoring their work.

Counter-mapping

Participants were given the option to take a subversive role and beat the system. Three subgroups did so. One developed a program of *Scatter Tags*: these small chips would be randomly scattered throughout public space to send out false signals and upset the system. One subgroup focussed on a privacy application and proposed a sort of cape that would blur any signal following them. Subgroup *Big Sister* turned the tables around by using the living map to track authorities. Highly placed officials, such as the Minister of Security, would be tracked by members of the network, and even more members would be drafted through live broadcasting to get an even more precise image of the person. Video footage is presented to the person in question in order to warn and frighten them.

Interestingly enough, these roles were all taken by participants who were security experts themselves. They appeared to be the most concerned about possible privacy infringement due to the living map. Also, they perceived the role of hackers essential in the development of a living map: they are the counterforce that points out the weak spots in the system.

34
.TAG

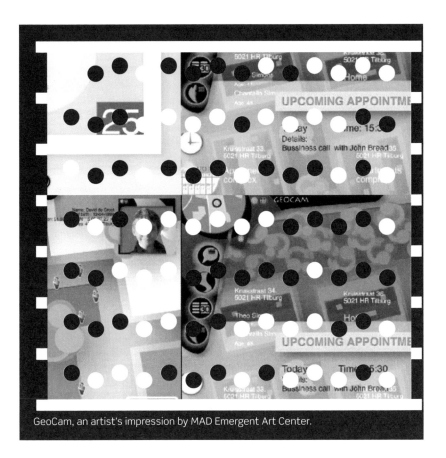

GeoCam, an artist's impression by MAD Emergent Art Center.

Big Brother: from Orwell to Endemol

Big Brother has been given new meaning over the last decade and this shows an interesting shift in people's perception of privacy. It started in 1949 as a fictitious dictator in George Orwells novel 1984. Orwell demonstrated how the combination of collective goals and technology will corrupt into a system that crushes individual freedom. Like the panoptic model, the state of Oceania was controlled by surveillance cameras and bill boards warning people that 'Big Brother is watching you'. During privacy debates in the decades that followed, this scenario was often cited as a warning against communism and fascism.

Since 1999, Big Brother is increasingly associated with a television format developed by Dutch entertainment company Endemol. In the Big Brother reality soap, people are locked up in a house for hundred days, surveyed 24/7 and awarded with votes from the television audience. Due to its success, the format got many international versions and variants such as *The Real World, Expedition Robinson and The Golden Cage*. Participants do not seem to care about their privacy and go to great lengths to win the favour of the public, for example, by gossiping, flirting, fighting or eating cockroaches. Big Brother, once a warning against totalitarianism, now has become a symbol of the importance of being known.

0110 .0100 Managing Identities on the Living Map

The design sessions showed how various people perceive a future living map as a logical next step in this information society. People are able to envision how live, location-based data can empower them. Many participants also demonstrated the urge to connect as much personal information as possible into a single device, while they discovered afterwards that information will need to be collected, filtered and presented. But by whom? Here we discern a sense of Identity Management among participants, although none actually used the term.

Building up a profile is seen as inevitable: this will state your preferences, serve as a filter and connect you to like-minded others. Much is expected from other users who provide each other reviews and are connected on the basis of their profiles. Most participants trust governments to provide objective information or even state that governments have a right to use personal data already collected on them, as it is their data. Businesses are trusted less, but they may come up with more innovative solutions, connecting needs among different users and providing a platform for self-organisation. Still, users should also have the option to change their profiles if they provide unwanted results, and also have an option to remain anonymous.

During the discussions within the different groups, we observed a difference between lay people among the groups of randomly selected citizens and legal, political or technological experts selected from conferences and ministries. The lay people would sigh that privacy is just a thing of the past and you need to live with the fact everything is known about you. Personalisation is seen as the default setting, anonymity as an option for the few who want it. Experts would argue privacy is a fundamental right and it needs to be built into the system as the default setting. Especially when it comes to security, lay people tended towards an all-knowing state – some even feeling more secure while being watched. Experts warned for the rise of a totalitarian state and argued for building in more checks and balances.

Although all participants agree that the living map will be inevitable and Identity Management will be problematic, they differ on whether the scenario is desirable. Privacy is the biggest obstacle for some, while many others argue that empowerment itself may as well be our biggest enemy. In our urge to use data to live life as we want it, we may be developing a system that turns daily events into calculable, predictable, efficient and customised experiences. Some of the experts see many advantages here: the living map serves as a platform for bringing together the needs of everyone in a harmonious way. Many others, especially among the lay people, argue that we may lose something that makes us human: adventure, intuition, spontaneity. They don't want to live like robots in a mechanised world. Perhaps sometimes it may also be good to meet someone who does not match your profile.

0110 .0101 Conclusions

Participants of the sessions generally found the scenario of a living map quite plausible, as it should and will provide users empowerment. The lay participants generally perceived privacy as something from the past. Most experts, however, argued that it is a basic right. Proposals were put forward for building in a sense of forgetfulness into the data storage. Still, they do understand that they should build up a profile somehow in order to filter information and manage who is going to get access to it. Information systems need to gather personal information in order to work, but we should avert a situation in which everyone can watch everyone. Businesses should adhere to privacy guidelines, while law enforcement should be able to track everyone in case of emergency. Without using the term, they understood the notion of Identity Management.

Still, the most common fear that participants shared concerned the net changing what it means to be human: we might lose spontaneity and substitute adventure for efficiency and predictability. In sum, the living map is perceived as handy and inevitable, but people just do not want to live like robots. The system should therefore always contain a button for checking out again, although few believe this button will really exist in the future.

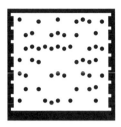

TAG for note 1

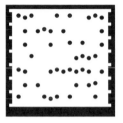

TAG for note 2

Notes

1 The sessions with citizens were held in meeting rooms, with the civil servants at their offices and with the experts during conferences. One session was held in Shanghai with an international Group, the rest in the Netherlands.

2 Sessions were moderated and analysed by Christian van 't Hof and Floortje Daemen. Johan Hoogeveen helped with the registration and analysis of several sessions.

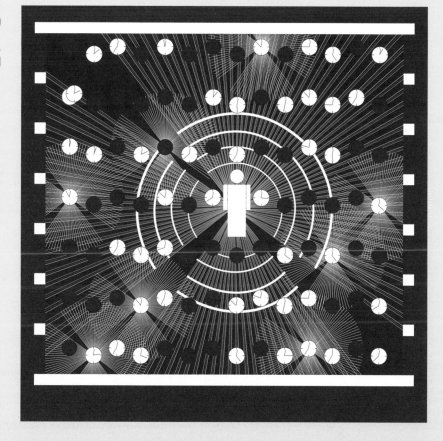

Conclusions

Identity Management
in the Net

Rinie van Est and Christian van 't Hof

'You can check out any

time you like, but you can

never leave.'

Design Principles for Living *in* the Net

This book shows how the digital and physical worlds are increasingly interweaving and how we, in our daily movements through public space, continuously check in and out. We are shifting from being *on* the net to being *in* the net. This has a large influence on the way in which we, as citizens, (will) experience and make use of public space. Through all sorts of devices we give away numbers that say things about us, and in exchange we get access to information, spaces, services and goods. Our digital identities are becoming increasingly valuable, but who exactly governs the system is becoming less and less clear, while the system's goals frequently seem to shift. With that, Identity Management becomes a handful for everyone.

In this final chapter we list all the technological trends that make a development to *in* the net possible, what the social implications of this new phase in our information society are, and the roles that citizens can play themselves in managing their identities. The concept Identity Management has been described in the introduction as a combination between *privacy* and *empowerment*. Privacy is a basic right, protected according to the Fair Information Principles, as described in the first chapter. However, citizens also want to make good use of the information that the new systems in public space collect and process. From the perspective of empowerment, we define the roles of (groups of) citizens in dealing with personal data.

The Netherlands has its own particular way of going in the net: there is a strong belief in large information systems to solve many problems, coupled with an open and lively debate among many stakeholders. This makes the Dutch situation ideal for learning lessons on how governments, businesses and citizens give shape to data systems and deal with the use and management of personal data. We also contrasted the different Dutch case studies to comparable systems in Europe, Asia and the US. Finally, we kept in touch with users of these systems through the design sessions.

Drawing on this diversity of systems, stakeholder opinions and cultural contexts, we come to twelve design principles for Identity Management *in* the net.

The Technology from *on* to *in* the Net

For a long time, the digital world was separate from the physical world – cyberspace and electronic highways had nothing to do with public space and asphalt roads. Around the turn of the century, most people in developed countries were *on* the net. The past decade, four technological trends have become apparent, which show that they are going from being *on* the net to being *in* the net. The first trend is the visible appearance of digital devices in public space: from ticket machines to cameras, digital wicket gates, GPS and mobile phones. These devices add unique numbers to objects, events and people, building up a digital identity while you move through public space. CCTV made its first appearance in the 1990s. Mobile phones only had their breakthrough at the start of this century and TomTom is also something from recent years. Contactless smart cards in public transport can currently be used in most large cities around the world. The devices to check in and out exchange information and link it to a specific place and time. They do not only register that something has been paid, viewed or that a call has been made, but also where it happened and when.

Digital devices pass on this data through networks that are increasingly fusing together. Digital convergence is the second trend. This can be seen best in mobile telephones: GPRS, UMTS, RFID, Wi-Fi, Bluetooth and GPS all come together in the same device. Also with road traffic, loads of data congregates – from meanders in the road, cameras by the road, signals from mobiles and satellite navigation systems – thrown together they form an overall picture of traffic. Thus, we are speaking of a network of networks. Next to this, there is a strong inclination to link all this information to the internet: the net of nets. Consequently, the 'Internet of Things' has become the most commonly used term for this development: all sorts of vehicles, cards, mobiles and consumer products receive a separate IP address[1], get connected to the internet and thereby form a network of things.

Thirdly, more and more information on the net is getting a spatial and temporal dimension. We are heading in the direction of so-called *mirror worlds*.[2] Services such as Google Earth have made satellite imagery, aerial photographs and street photographs of our world available and digitally searchable through the internet. Moreover, they offer a virtual platform for all sorts of services. Increasingly, data on objects, people and events include X, Y and T (time) coordinates. Here we enter the field of geo-data, which was once a small academic branch and which is now one of the hottest topics at IT conferences. Combining these data on the map, the abovementioned scenario of *Living Maps* becomes a reality.

Fourthly, internet, and thereby the above services, has become available in many more places, especially through smartphones, laptops and netbooks. In just a short time, many urban areas have become covered by a network of antennae, while the Netherlands is almost fully covered as a country. With the changeover from GPRS to UMTS and WIMAX, the bandwidth of these networks increased. The speed of data exchange which was, until recently, only possible from behind a desk, is now almost always available, almost anywhere in public space. This does not only make it possible to deliver more data, it also makes it possible for people to communicate through images, not just sound. Soon, more people will make use of location markers through NFC, matrix codes and GPS coordinates, turning their phone into a mouse to click on and read their environment. Subsequently, information will be increasingly location-based and displayed on maps, such as Google Earth and TomTom, connecting cyberspace to the here and now.

Does this complete the circle; has the net closed in on us? No, not yet, and the question is if this will ever happen. The developments described here are trends and not endpoints. The net doesn't cover everywhere; it contains many gaps. Sometimes these gaps have been chosen consciously because of privacy reasons or because complete netting is not cost-effective. The time factor is relative, too. The clocks of the devices are not always completely synchronised and many nets slow down because data in transfer is buffered. Even if all data is available live, it will not always be seen by someone, because there is simply too much to see. However, the four trends do contribute to a feeling and an expectation that everything is always and everywhere connected to the net.

Futurists such as Ray Kurzweil (2005) use the term 'singularity' to mark the point in history when computers, through exponential development in computing speeds, will become smarter than people.[3] One of the critiques on this notion is that mankind is capable of much more than only processing data; we have feelings and intuition, whereby a computer will never outsmart a human. From the perspective of the digitalisation of public space, we could adapt Kurzweils perspective and call it 'network singularity': the point where all networks are connected and machines are better networked than humans. Gerard van Oortmerssen states that from the perspective of a single worldwide network, two future scenarios are conceivable. In the first scenario, the intelligent network increases our knowledge and power, which in turn creates a stronger social network and a collective consciousness. In the second scenario, technology develops itself to a superior new 'species' (in Darwin terminology) which will start to lead its own life and ultimately dominate mankind.[4]

Computers may not surpass man in individual capacities to act, but they will surpass us in the way in which we are networked. We therefore need an open discussion about how the architecture of this net must evolve and agree upon a set of design principles. First of all, this is to prevent one group of users from dominating public space over others, but perhaps also to enable us humans to govern the net instead of the net governing us.

Identity Management *in* the Net

What is the meaning of the development from *on* the net to *in* the net for the privacy debate? In order to interpret this question we looked at the history of the privacy debate at the beginning of this book. The privacy debate stems from the 1970s, but with the rise of the internet it got another face in the 1990s. The theme of the privacy debate in the 1970s was Big Brother; fear for misuse of personal data between citizen and state. Citizens supplied personal data for the pleasure of the welfare state. In the 1990s we went *on* the net which posed us two extra challenges. Markets and citizens check in by themselves. Personal data has become an important medium of exchange for the free obtainment of certain commercial services.[5] Citizens do not only share personal data with the government or markets in exchange for services, but also consciously produce personal data and make this publicly available on the internet, as can be seen on social networking sites such as Facebook, MySpace and LinkedIn. Interestingly enough, it is often the market that makes this possible (usually free of charge). Managing personal data is thereby not only a matter of fear for misuse; the wish to generate personal data and make it available is characteristic of our time.

Therefore, the concept of Identity Management is more suitable for this time: a combination of the protection of personal data (*privacy*) and the wish for self-realisation (*empowerment*). The concepts of privacy and empowerment are connected in various ways. Firstly, the basic right for privacy is regulated in such a way that citizens are able to develop themselves in relatively unconstrained and autonomous ways. The right for privacy is principally empowering to the individual. Protection of personal data is legally covered through the Fair Information Principles; in case of the Netherlands the Data Protection Act (DPA), which is monitored by the Dutch Data Protection Authority. Still, these principles offer all too meagre prospects for the wishes and the skills of modern citizens. We therefore

What kind of numbers are attached to you?

use empowerment as a supplementary perspective that can give us insights into how people wish to deal with their personal data.

In the following four sections we will describe in what ways the right to privacy is protected when we start living *in* the net. The privacy principles form the legal starting point of this debate. These principles encourage the collection and processing of personal data happens with utmost care. How do they give meaning to its guidelines, such as purpose specification and limitation to data collection, *in* the net? We also look at *in* the net from a citizen empowerment standpoint. From this perspective, the laws and institutions do not play a central role; it is the skills and wishes of citizens that matter. We look at a citizen in his role of inquirer and user of information, manager of his identity, co-designer of systems and services, and requester for security. These roles can be seen in the four central topics that we will cover: use of personal data, management of personal data, design of IT systems and use of personal data for criminal investigation. With each theme we will formulate a number of design principles (see box below) from the perspectives of the protection of personal data and empowerment.

Design principles for Identity Management *in* the net

Use of personal data

1. Safeguard citizens' anonymity in public space as much as possible.
2. Let citizens, too, profit from their own personal data.
3. Promote access to (government) data.

Management of personal data

4. Provide good, institutional management of personal data.
5. Make use of the knowledge and social engagement of hackers.
6. Heighten the amount of control that citizens have over their own digital identities.

Design of IT systems

7. Keep identities as separate and revocable as possible.
8. Involve citizens with determining system requirements and the development of new services.
9. Let old systems run alongside new ones.
10. Avoid too much systematism.

Use of personal data for criminal investigation

11. Make clear under what circumstances the right to anonymity can be revoked.
12. Consider the costs and benefits of the investigation with regard to the goal and the infringement of privacy.

Use of Personal Data: Limitations and Giving Access

Especially with the use of personal data, empowerment offers a radically different viewpoint than the protection of personal data (see table below) does. In protecting privacy, limiting the use of personal data is central. The thought behind it is: the less data that is being registered, the less misuse can be made of it; the so-called Collection Limitation Principle. This principle is immediately applicable to the protection of personal data in public space, fulfilling the desire to safeguard the anonymity of citizens in public space as much as possible. Only when national security is at stake, this right can be withdrawn. However, citizens do not always wish to remain anonymous in public space; they sometimes want to be recognised and known. The empowerment perspective gives attention to users' needs to have control of their personal data and make themselves visible to others. Important design principles that come into play here are as follows: let citizens, too, profit from their own personal data, and give them access to (government) data.

Starting points and design principles for the use of personal data

Perspective	Safeguarding personal data	Empowerment
Starting points	Dealing with informational inequality.	Public request for informational equality.
	Citizens' rights to privacy (constitution, DPA).	Citizens' rights to access to government data.
Design principles	1 Safeguard citizens' anonymity in public space as much as possible.	2 Let citizens, too, profit from their own personal data.
		3 Promote access to (government) data.

1   Safeguard citizens' anonymity in public space as much as possible
Limitation to data collection is a well-known way to avoid misuse of
personal data. The different cases in this book show that the application
of this principle for use of data systems in public space often refers to
the safeguarding of the anonymity of citizens in (digital) public space.
This principle is brought forward most clearly at screen captures of individuals in public space; such as through CCTV and Google Street View.
For example, a local government act ensures that anyone captured on
CCTV not committing an offence will remain anonymous. Identification
only takes place in the case of criminal investigation. After a public outcry,
Google Street View used face-blurring technology to make people unrec-
ognisable. This solution is not waterproof. In certain cases, citizens can
ask Google to remove unwanted images.

Anonymity is also important when moving through public space.
The Telecommunications Act only allows the processing of location data
if it is made anonymous. This is why TomTom cuts the beginning and end
off each route; so data cannot lead back to specific addresses. With contactless smart cards in public transport, a passenger's anonymity is not
possible in the Netherlands if they have a discount or season pass, while
the Hong Kong Octopus card does: it only defines you as a student, elder
or child and it is only personalised if you asked for it. The need for anonymous travel as a default setting will probably be a central theme at the
privacy discussion on pay-as-you-drive, too. There are innumerable ways
in which this principle can be embedded in the yet-to-be-built Dutch dynamic
road pricing system, for example with prepayment or with an option to
keep using the old way of road taxing next to the new one.

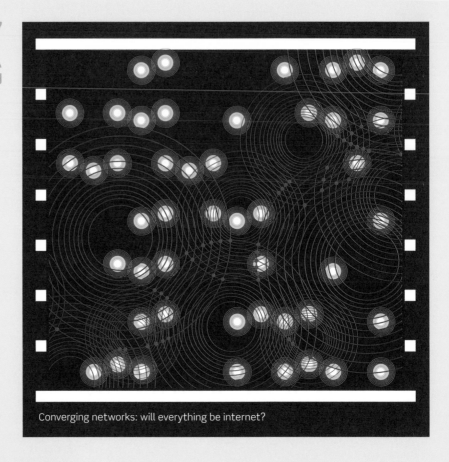

Converging networks: will everything be internet?

2 Let citizens, too, profit from their own personal data

Many users welcome the advantages that information technology can offer them through their personal data. Think in terms of convenience, discounts to services or information. A good example would be a localisation service, such as Foursquare or Google Latitude. Instead of being anonymous, users of these services actually want to let certain people know where they are. The parallels with social networks on the web are apparent, but a spatial component has been added. Using this information, it is also possible to map your own behaviour: the *life-logging* trend.

The different systems that have been described offer numerous potential services for the advantage of users. In case of digitalised public transport, companies could offer a *best-pricing system*, with which passengers gain insights in the cheapest way to travel. Current satellite navigation systems offer technical options for letting your friends know where you are at a given moment, as Kolman demonstrates with her Networked Car experiment.[6] Choosing for such a service is not obligatory; it is a choice. In offering users more chances of using the data that becomes available to them through various data systems; they, too, can profit from their own personal data which is being collected by public or private organisations. Moreover, this enlarges the basis for introducing new systems.

3   Promote access to (government) data

Technologies such as the internet, Google Earth and TomTom are being embraced by users, because they make data accessible to everyone in an easy, affordable way. From the perspective of empowerment, sharing data is an important design principle. Until now, mostly private parties have ensured this. The government also does this, but could do more. Concerning contactless smart cards in public transport, the Netherlands has a national, publicly accessible database with real-time traffic data planned out. The networked car shows that in the field of traffic data, private parties cooperating with the National Data Warehouse for Traffic Information (NDW) delivered a real-time data system. Still, there is a lot of public data that is difficult to access. The European INSPIRE guideline therefore requests governments to take an active role in making available any geographical data to other parties.[7]

Personal Data Management: Institutional Management and Individual Management

The second subject concerns safe management of personal data in order to avoid misuse by third parties. Institutions can play a role in this, but also users. Different principles apply for the organisations that are responsible for the management of personal data. According to the Data Quality Principle, personal data collected should be relevant to the purposes for which they are to be used, and when used it should be accurate, complete, and kept up-to-date. The Security Safeguards Principle is aimed at security measures to minimise the risk of unauthorised access, destruction, use, modification or disclosure of personal data. Finally, the Openness Principle states that the collection of data should happen in a transparent way to the user. What these principles do not cover is how citizens can play a role in managing personal data. Moreover, they do not take into account the important role played by socially active computer scientists, who provide a service to our society when they exhibit the weak points of a data system in a timely manner.

Starting points and design principles for the management
of personal data

Perspective	Safeguarding personal data	Empowerment
Starting points	Fight damage from data, such as identity theft. Security by security experts and frequent privacy audits.	A citizen as protector and manager of his dynamic identity. The power of civil disobedience.
Design principles	4 Provide good, institutional management of personal data.	5 Make use of the knowledge and social engagement of hackers. 6 Enhance the amount of control that citizens have over their own digital identities.

4 Provide good, institutional management of personal data

Good, institutional management demands the security of personal data and the transparency of the way in which it is managed. The cases show various ways in which similar data protection principles are anchored. The providers of satellite navigation appear successful in the implementation of the limitation principle, for example through chopping off the first and last piece of every route and through applying encryption. The Limitation Principle appeared to be problematic with contactless smart cards in public transport and CCTV. With contactless smart cards, public transport companies are obliged to have a privacy audit performed every two years and inform the Dutch Data Protection Authority of the results. Moreover, the government, prompted by social organisations and the Dutch DPA, asked these companies to establish a code of conduct. This code shows that there is no research into travelling behaviour, marketing or issuing data to third parties, unless the passenger has explicitly given permission for this. Nevertheless, due to the continuous changes in the guidelines and the shifts between opt-in and opt-out rules, it is still unclear to passengers who follow them.

In case of camera surveillance, a specific legislation was deemed necessary. CCTV was seen as a technological innovation with possible huge consequences for the privacy of citizens in public space. Within society and politics, a gradual, yet great need arose for clarity on how camera images ought to be handled. Therefore, a specific legislation was developed for CCTV that gives citizens the right to see the images, know when they were filmed, and have specific images removed, amongst other things. In practice, however, it appears that a large number of municipalities do not actually offer these possibilities.

Concerning pay-as-you-drive and Near Field Communication, the discussion on the institutional protection of personal data has yet to commence. Considering the experiences with CCTV, it seems wise to develop separate statutory regulations for pay-as-you-drive. Where CCTV is local and concerns demarcated public areas, dynamic road pricing will cover the entire country. Even more than with CCTV, therefore, this is about a large, technical system with potentially massive consequences for privacy. In case of NFC, additional regulation may not be necessary once it is clear who is actually managing the personal data, the so-called Accountability Principle. A Trusted Service Manager may as well fall under the current banking and telecommunication rules, as long as it is clear the this party is accountable for handling the data.

5 Make use of the knowledge and social engagement of hackers

No data system can be one hundred per cent secure; every code can be hacked. However, it is certainly useful to design systems in such a way that the effort that has to be made to hack the code is larger than the yield. Moreover, procedures ought to be developed just in case the system does get broken into. In order to achieve this, it is important to subject the system from the start to so-called 'white hat' or ethical hackers. These socially responsible hackers distinguish themselves from the bad guys through an important principle: if you are able to hack the system, you will first notify the organisation responsible, so they can take measures.

In this way, security experts of the Digital Security Group of Radboud University showed that various RFID systems based on the MiFare Classic chip can be hacked. Because this chip is not only used for the Dutch public transport contactless smart card but also in important government buildings, the group brought the news with utmost care. First the authorities and the owners of the systems were notified and precautions could be taken – within the system itself and within the organisation behind it. Malicious hackers could have gained access to the buildings by hacking the chips, or begun circulating fake smart cards. Because of the work of the Digital Security Group, the chip in the cards was replaced with more secure chips and all sorts of fraud detection mechanisms were set in place in the back office.

The race between security experts and hackers carries on, undiminished. And the bigger the interest of the system, the bigger the attraction for hackers – both the benevolent as well as the malicious ones. If the dynamic road pricing system will ever gain ground, it will become a strong magnet for hackers. Openness between the authorities and companies who will manage the system, including the white hat hackers, will be of great importance.

6 Enhance the amount of control that citizens have over their own digital identities

The digital identities of citizens are only partially protected by the DPA. For example, the act gives citizens insights into collected data, but in practice, it is frequently unclear who knows what about you and what this person does with this knowledge. Also, citizens do not have a right to see in what way their digital identity gets established. Options for citizens to manage their identities themselves are limited. In this way, the legal demands of the DPA frequently lead to illegible end-user license agreements, which users do not read, but simply check for the sake of agreeing. Thereby providers adhere to the law, while citizens do not know what they are up against, let alone that they can decide what does and what doesn't get told about them. It is important that users are able to make the right choices concerning how people handle their personal data. Incomprehensible juridical texts will not help citizens with this.

The so-called Privacy Coach (see case study *Money Mobiles*) is an innovative concept designed to help users with negotiating the use of their personal data. Based on a questionnaire, the user builds his own profile and the Privacy Coach will indicate if this profile matches the provider of services. In case of a mismatch, the user can enter a discussion with the provider. If the coach provides a match, users can be assured that whatever happens to their personal data is alright with them.

The case studies show that users especially like convenience and

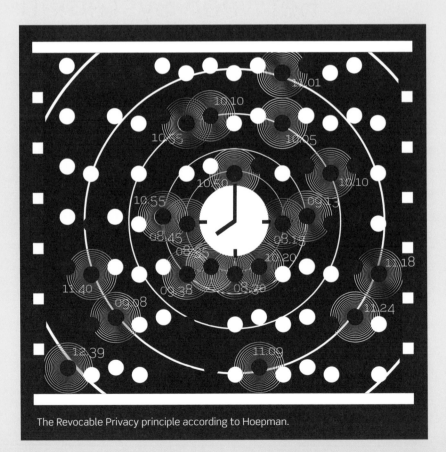

The Revocable Privacy principle according to Hoepman.

basically trust that everything is well-designed. They usually only take action when something goes wrong. This is why citizens must be capable of erasing their digital identities in case that they do not agree with the identity that they have built. Sometimes this is arranged by law. For example, the Data Protection Act states that citizens can have CCTV images erased. However, this option is not always offered in every municipality and not every citizen is aware of it. Google Street View also offers an option to have images erased, although there, too, you will not always know what others are already seeing of you.

Even less visible for citizens are the identities that they build in databases. Linking databases revolves mostly around numbers. Through the invisibility of these numbers, citizens only see that something is wrong when transactions do not work, when they receives unwanted advertising, or when they is suspected of doing something they did not do. In such cases, citizens ought to be able to erase their digital identities and start afresh. However, this is only possible if these identities are technically and organisationally sufficiently separate, thereby enabling them to be changed or erased (see design principle 7).

IT System Design: Between Systematism and Alternatives

Data system architecture is politics: the design of (and choice for) IT systems is not only about economics and technique, but also about Identity Management. An important starting point of the DPA is that the organisation responsible for managing a database may not use the personal data for other purposes than why it was collected in the first place. This is the Purpose Specification Principle. In order to put this principle into practice and somewhat maintain it, it is important that various identities can be recalled or erased. Next to countering unwanted functional shifts, wanted functional developments ought to be made possible as well.

Users can fulfil an important role in determining the social requirements that a system needs to meet; they are frequently the source of new services. From the perspective of user-friendliness, it is often desirable that citizens will always be able to choose between various systems. In practice this means that old systems will continue to exist next to new systems for a long time. A design principle that is very important from the perspective of empowerment is the avoidance of systematism. This phenomenon occurs when a system architecture compels users to act in a certain way, often sneaking up on them unwanted.

Starting points and design principles for the design and use of IT systems

Perspective	Safeguarding personal data	Empowerment
Starting points	Privacy as legal precondition.	Users as co-designers of the system.
	Counter unwanted functional shifts (Purpose Specification Principle).	Making possible desired functional developments.
Design principles	7 Keep identities as separate and revocable as possible.	8 Involve citizens with determining system requirements and the development of new services.
		9 Let old systems run alongside new ones.
		10 Avoid too much systematism.

7   Keep identities as separate and revocable as possible

If you check in on the net, a unique number is sent to a database which leads to your digital identity in that system. This number is random, in principle, but it is frequently linked to numbers which are not easily substituted: address, date of birth or a national identification number. This makes it easier to link files, which will provide more information on you and consequently optimise service. However, at the same time, it makes it harder to switch identities, in case your identity is not right, stolen, or for any other reason unwanted.

The 16-digit number on Dutch public transport cards, the numbers in your mobile telephone or your email account are, in essence, random numbers. If your card gets hacked frequently or you suddenly get a lot of unwanted advertising, your number can be exchanged for another one and you begin a new digital identity. With traffic jam detection in the Tom-Tom system, the temporary nature of numbers is programmed in already: your car will be assigned a new number time and time again and thereby builds but a minimal identity. The number is there to identify you as someone who drives in a certain place at a certain speed, and not who you are. Like this, facets of your digital identity are not only technically separable, but also organisationally. Only the organisation responsible for the management of the system has access to what hides behind the number. According to the same line of thinking, databases with personal data and transaction data of NFC services could be separated and adaptable too.

Other numbers are often less changeable and thereby cause people to build a richer digital identity over time, across various systems, such as addresses or a vehicle registration number. A national identification number is the most permanent identity number that citizens have: this number is unique and remains the same from birth to death; all systems in which you are registered with this number could in theory be linked. A reserved approach to using this number is therefore advisable. If something goes wrong with this, the citizen concerned can have problems the rest of his life.

8   Involve citizens with determining system requirements and the development of new services

The different case studies show that Dutch citizens (individuals and in groups) like to let their voices be heard, answer if a certain system should be introduced at all, and determine the design requirements for the system. With CCTV, in about half of the cases there had been some consultation with neighbours. In three-quarters of these municipalities, citizens voted for the introduction of CCTV. The development of NFC in the key mobile went hand in hand with user tests and public surveys by Rabo Mobile in the Dutch Midlands and by Payter in Rotterdam. Dynamic road pricing sparked political unrest concerning the internet survey of the ANWB and its import for political decision-making processes. Some Dutch parties even suggested to let the introduction of dynamic road pricing be determined by a referendum.[8] It makes quite a bit of difference for what kind of system you vote 'yes' or 'no'. This is why it is important to, in an early phase, involve citizens and social organisations with the design of a system.

A role that is still somewhat underexposed is the role of citizens as devisers or even (co-)developers of new services. During the emergence of internet and mobile telephones, users themselves appeared to play an important role in innovation. The emergence of SMS and Wikipedia has been brought about by users. The challenge is to make use of the gigantic innovation potential that users have, especially now we are going *in* the net. The design sessions on the *Living Map* demonstrated the citizens are ready for it.

9   Let old systems run alongside new ones

While in almost all shops in the Netherlands you can pay by bank card, you can also pay cash, or through other electronic systems. A new application such as NFC will only become successful if users truly find a use for it. It is a matter of providing enough choice: space for new applications, without users immediately having to discard the old one. However, this does lead to the consequence that promised new systems take longer to prove themselves.

With contactless smart cards and pay-as-you-drive, the wish to have new systems run alongside the old ones is under great pressure; these two systems only seem to work optimally when other systems are excluded. For example, the contactless smart card system can only completely calculate the income and expenses of carriers when other payment methods have been abolished. The system only gives a total overview of the passenger streams when all passengers check in and out. The gates at the station can only bar fare dodgers if there is no other way of getting onto the platform. It is therefore understandable that the providers of the system are in a bit of a hurry with abolishing the old system. From a passenger's point of view this hurry is much less comprehensible. He enjoys having choices. Letting two different systems exist alongside one another is also a gauge to the provider of the success of the system. Only when the majority of passengers switch to the new system, the old system can be abolished. Therefore, the consumer's union and Rover plead for a dual system. Japan, too, where they have the saying 'the customer is God', has chosen for this approach. In this way, the system makes a friendlier impression to users, while it forces the provider to convince passengers of this particular system's added value.

The introduction of dynamic road pricing, too, poses the problem of switching from an existing to a new situation. How long will the Ministry of Transport, Public Works and Water Management allow for one driver to pay per kilometre and another to pay per year? Or should road users be able to choose themselves according to which system they pay?

10 Avoid too much systematism

Some of the information systems we have described can be used for the overt categorisation of citizens by states or business, leading in some cases to outcries of Big Brother accusations. Still, more subtle forms of systematism often escape our attention. Facial recognition in digital passports compels every citizen not to laugh upon having their passport photograph taken. This way we quietly lost something beautiful: freedom of expression. It is of utmost importance that citizens' freedom of expression in public space is preserved. Take dancing in the streets. A smart camera will detect this as aggressive behaviour and will send police to the location in question. It would be a great loss if, at some point, citizens become aware of these mechanisms and thereby suppress the urge to dance in the streets or boisterously embrace others. Such new forms of self-discipline because of the digitalisation of public space are unwanted.

The design sessions on the future image of the Living Map brought forward a different, modern form of systematism. We observed fierce discussions between participants on the correct balance between predictability and spontaneity. Advocates describe the advantages of the new data systems through a more efficient organisation of their daily lives. Opponents fear a 'computer-directed life', in other words, the automation of human existence. In his book with the telling title of *The Tomtomisation of the Passionate Human Being* (2006), Joep Schrijvers conveyed a similar message. He describes the rise of the so-called 'neologistic order'. In contrast to the form of systematism as described above, this does not concern a central power that forces something upon a user, but rather a decentralised power that users themselves can wield. The neologistic order is characterised by thinking in terms of utility; everything is subjected to goals to be achieved. In order to achieve a given goal, all sorts of data systems are used, that preferably keep users up to date in real-time on the changes in the environment, so that the path towards the desired goal can constantly be adjusted.[9] TomTom fits perfectly within the new neologistic order; especially the real-time navigation systems that are now being developed. In such systems, the destination is pre-programmed and current traffic data is collected and processed real-time, and based on this, adjustments are made to the optimal route.

The central question from the empowerment perspective is to what extent these kinds of data systems can help people to organise their lives better, or if they actually push them into a straightjacket of efficiency. Schrijvers states that those systems rob human beings of their existence: 'It has become out of the question to lead a life that is a succession of joyful and sad events that may overcome a person'.[10] Apparently, empowerment also has limits and can be its own enemy. FriendFinder increases the chance of getting back in touch with old friends, but perhaps decreases the chance of meeting new friends. The Child Safety Service in Japan pinpoints the location of a child in a neighbourhood to gives parents tranquillity of mind, but perhaps it also robs these same children of their much-needed freedom to develop themselves into independent adults through trial and error. In what ways do weather radars make our lives more pleasant, and where does this cybernetic system keep us from having a beautiful walk, if need be in the rain? Moreover, it might be necessary for our development as human beings to once in a while meet someone that does not match our profile.

Use of Personal Data for Criminal Investigation: Security and Privacy

In order to save victims, find witnesses and trace suspects, people need to be identified. When high security interests are at stake – a collective interest – citizens may lose their right to privacy temporarily. When security is at stake, the DPA is overruled by laws covering investigation. With new data systems it is not always clear what powers investigation services actually have. In those cases, the government ought to make clear in what situations and how investigation services may make use of data in those new systems. Revocable anonymity seems to be a suitable design principle that deals with the area of tension surrounding security and privacy. Also, investigations ought to happen cost-effectively and must be balanced with other important social values. This is why it is important that the costs and benefits of means of investigation are considered carefully with regard to the goal of the investigation (what type of crime has been committed?) and the infringement of privacy.

Starting points and design principles for the use of personal data for criminal investigation

Perspective	Safeguarding personal data	Empowerment
Starting points	The privacy (anonymity in public space) of law-abiding citizens is safeguarded. Citizens ought to know the jurisdiction of investigation services.	Investigations must happen cost-effectively and must be balanced with other important social values.
Design principles	11. Make clear under what circumstances the right to anonymity can be revoked.	12. Consider the costs and benefits of the investigation with regard to the goal and the infringement of privacy.

11 Make clear under what conditions the right to anonymity can be revoked

According to computer security expert Hoepman, the contrast between privacy and security does not have to be irreconcilable. He pleads for *revocable privacy*.[11] Not every citizen in the streets is constantly followed. Users of data systems receive a number with which they build their digital identity. The link between that number and the data which can instantly lead to the physical identity of the person (name, address, national identification number, registration number, picture) can be encrypted, and only under very strict provisions be released. A single party manages the system, with only anonymous numbers, while another party holds but the key between the number and the person. The police are the third party. They are authorised to get the key for this anonymous identity under certain conditions, for example if someone is suspected of murder. This way, the privacy of most users is guaranteed, while a small group of suspects can still be identified.

According to the design principle of revocable privacy or anonymity, networked drivers can get a number for settling bills for road usage and predicting traffic jams. If the car is used as a getaway car at a bank robbery, or if the driver speeds through a village at 200 kilometres per hour, the police will receive the key in order to retrieve the identity of the driver concerned. With contactless smart cards in public transport, the link between the 16-digit number and the name and the national identification number of the person in question can be encrypted and can only be released under clear conditions.

A similar protocol also offers an opportunity to discuss the conditions under which upholders of justice may receive the key, and to establish these conditions legally. Currently this is not the case; for each case data is supplied by the Prosecution Counsel, as was done in May 2007 with a rape in the Rotterdam underground (see case study *Gated Stations*). The fact that the Prosecution Counsel was able to supply this data, with the exception of passport photographs, forms important jurisprudence, which was litigated about for two years. It would have been better if Trans Link Systems directly let the carriers, passengers and investigation services known what they were up against.

Another example is automatic number plate recognition. Until the start of 2010, according to the Dutch Police Records Act (Wet politiegegevens), the registration numbers of drivers who have a clean record (the so called 'no hits': people who are not wanted by the police) could be stored for three days. The Dutch Data Protection Authority found that police forces in Rotterdam-Rijnmond and IJsselland broke this law. They saved all data for ten to over 100 days. The forces had concluded that the reprimand of the Dutch DPA was exaggerated. The government, in turn, adjusted the act by extending the storage time for non-suspect citizens to ten days. This way of handling the situation is debatable. In the many public surveys we see that citizens have a lot of trust in police use of data systems. Resolute violation of laws by the government itself impairs this trust.

The social discussion on the balance between privacy and investigation will become more important if it does not only cover the investigation of crime, but also the so-called preventative investigation; an investigation conducted already before a criminal offence has been committed. The General Intelligence and Security Service in the Netherlands (AIVD) does this more and more frequently in order to track organised crime or terrorists before they carry out their crimes. The case of automatic number plate recognition (ANPR) by the police is also a form of preventative investigation. Especially in such cases it is important to make clear, through a public and political debate, under what circumstances the right to anonymity can be revoked.

12 Consider the costs and benefits of the investigation with regard to the goal and the infringement of privacy

The social debate on powers of criminal investigation often covers the contrast between security and privacy. The Advisory Committee Security and Privacy from 2009, also called the Committee-Brouwer-Korf, states: do not collect more data than you need based on a risk analysis (proportionality) and use this data only for the goal for which permission was granted (goal commitment). The costs of an investigation also ought to be included in the discussion on costs and benefits of investigating. The data retention guidelines state that organisations responsible for managing data systems must save data on who communicated with whom, paid what and where, for one whole year, and they must be able to provide the police with this data within a quarter of an hour in a certain file format (see Chapter 1, *Living in the Net*). The costs for the adjustment of the systems and the provision of data are paid by the provider, and therefore indirectly by the user. This way it is unclear how much this security actually costs, let alone that it can be established whether the benefits outweigh the costs. The EU Data Retention guideline 2006 has been drafted for simple internet and telephone traffic, such as mobile telephone traffic, two computers that use the internet to make contact, or a switch transaction. Now we go *in* the net, our daily actions are increasingly digitalised and thereby fall under the Data Retention Act. Consequently, the costs for data retention have exploded. It is important to map this increase in costs and include this in discussions.

You Can Check out Here

You can check out any time you like, but you can never leave.
    The Eagles, *Hotel California*

The book *Check In / Check Out* shows that we are going *in* the net. Through innumerable devices and systems, from automatic number plate registration and smartphones to CCTV and satellite navigation systems, public space is becoming increasingly computerised. This causes 'an external shell of intelligence around the Earth'.[12] This digitalisation of public space signifies a new phase in our information society. In this chapter we have examined the social implications of this development through the lens of Identity Management, as well as the role that citizens can play themselves. In order to give direction to the way that the government, businesses and citizens can deal with the digitalisation of public space, twelve design principles have been described for Identity Management *in* the net. What kind of general image does this exercise generate? How do the different design principles relate to each other? And to what extent does Identity Management differ between *in* the net and *on* the net?

The privacy discussion broadened with the emergence of the internet. Next to the protection against misuse of personal data, the use of personal data had become important to the government, businesses and citizens. The wish to promote the internal market through making an (international) exchange of data possible was granted with the Fair Information Principles, which prescribes how personal data needs to be carefully managed. With Identity Management *in* the net, we can see a number of familiar principles return. The phase of society *in* the net, however, is characterised by more data streams: every aspect of our daily lives, and where and when we are in public space, is digitalised. This way, the implementation of basic principles such as goal commitment, limiting use of personal data, and good security, have become more complex and harder to introduce and enforce (see design principles 1, 4 and 7). A part of the solution can be found in the empowerment perspective. We plead for a raise in citizen control over their own identities and the inclusion of citizens in deciding the requirements to which data systems must adhere (design principles 6 and 8). The security of these systems, too, can benefit from the social concern of hackers (design principle 5).

The shift from *on* the net to *in* the net probably comes forward most in design principle 1: Safeguard citizens' anonymity in public space as much as possible. The protection of privacy is a basic right, also in public space, so citizens may develop themselves autonomously and without constraints. This right can be revoked when security interests are at stake. The new data systems in public space offer plenty of opportunities for maintaining order and (preventative) investigation. However, the end does not justify all means. There is a need for a public and political discussion on the conditions under which a citizen's anonymity in public space may be revoked (design principle 11). We also plead for weighing the costs and benefits of (preventative) investigation against the goal and the infringement on privacy (design principle 12).

The above discussion on privacy and security indicates that the relationships between the various design principles are not free of tension. Principles that are set up from the perspective of personal data protection may be at odds with certain empowerment principles. Citizens do not only wish to remain anonymous in public space, they also want to show where they are and who they are. We are speaking of a Web 2.0 that has received a spatial component. This social web, or the 'internet of people', stretches across public space. Citizens, too, want to profit from the data that other parties are collecting on them in this public space, as well as from all the other (government) data that is available in this space (design principles 2 and 3).

However, even empowerment has its limits. The new data systems that span public space offer citizens innumerable possibilities and plenty of room to organise their lives and fully enjoy public space. At the same time, these cybernetic systems have a tendency to impose new kinds of social constraints on people (design principle 10). In the field of investigation, Bart Schermer sees a development from an 'architecture of observation' to an 'architecture of control', which will have a negative impact on the autonomy of citizens moving through public space.[13] But businesses (personalised advertising) and we ourselves (think TomTom, FriendFinder), too, wish to make use of the options for control that IT offers in public space. It is therefore important to make sure that all these digital relations do not keep us from connecting to our fellow citizens in the street. We lost a large part of public space years ago with the emergence of cars and slowly we are winning it back through limiting traffic in inner cities and through car-free Sundays. Let us make sure that digitalisation enriches public space, and that there will be no need in ten years to vote for a digi-free Sunday.

This concludes our joint journey through digitalised public space. You may now check out. Or is that no longer possible?

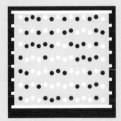

TAG for note 1

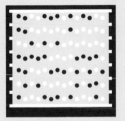

TAG for note 6

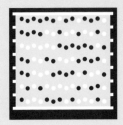

TAG for note 7

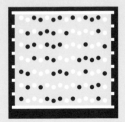

TAG for note 11

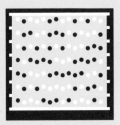

TAG for note 13

Notes

1 The current Ipv4 does not provide enough unique
   identities for that, but with Ipv6 we will have
   a virtually inexhaustible number of internet
   addresses available.

2 Castranova, E. et al. (2007). *Metaverse roadmap:
   Pathways to the 3D web*. Mountain View – Ca:
   Acceleration Studies Foundation.

3 Kurzweil, R. (2005). *The singularity is near: When
   humans transcend biology*. London: Viking Penguin.

4 Oortmerssen, G. van (2009). Darwin en het internet.
   (oration) Tilburg: Universiteit van Tilburg, p. 39.

5 Anderson, C. (2009). *Free: The future of a radical price*.
   New York: Hyperion Books.

6 http://bliin.com/

7 http://inspire.jrc.ec.europa.eu/

8 Vendrik, K. (2010). 'Een goed idee, die kilometerheffing? Ja, anders lopen we hopeloos vast'.
   NRC Next, 1 February 2010.

9 Schrijvers, J.P.M. (2006). *Het wilde vlees:
   De tomtomisering van de passionele mens*.
   Schiedam: Scriptum.

10 Idem Schrijvers, J.P.M. (2006), p. 187.

11 Hoepman, J.H. (2008). 'Revocable privacy'.
   Informatiebeveiliging, no. 5, pp. 14-17.

12 Idem Oortmerssen, G. van (2009).

13 Schermer, B.W. (2009). 'Surveillance and privacy in
   the ubiquitous network society'. *The Amsterdam
   Law Forum*, vol. 1, no. 4 (63-76), p. 68.

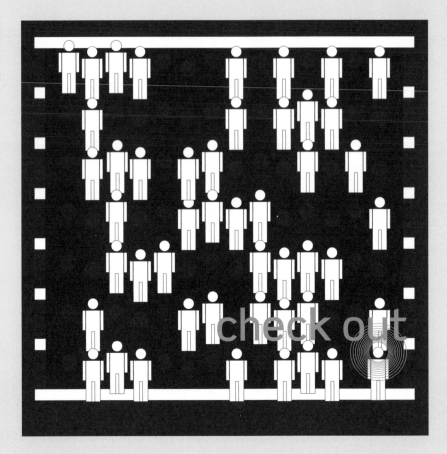

About the Authors

Floortje Daemen

Within the Technology Assessment department of the Rathenau Institute, Daemen does research on the digitalisation of public space as well as robotics. She has a background in Arts and Science studies and architectural engineering. Preceding her work at the Technology Assessment department, she worked at the Science System Assessment department of the Rathenau Institute.

f.daemen@rathenau.nl

Rinie van Est

Rinie van Est is a coordinator and 'trend-catcher' in the Technology Assessment (TA) department of the Rathenau Institute. He is a physicist and political scientist. He works on TA methods and technologies such as nanotechnology, robotics and Ambient Intelligence. Moreover, he teaches at the sub-faculty Technical Innovation Sciences at the Eindhoven University of Technology.

q.vanest@rathenau.nl

Christian van 't Hof

As a sociologist and electrical engineer, Van 't Hof researches the correlations between human and digital networks. He has done this as a researcher at the Ithaca Media Group, RAND Europe, and since 2004, at the Rathenau Institute. Furthermore, he presents popular scientific programmes.

c.vanthof@rathenau.nl

Jolanda Koffijberg

Jolanda Koffijberg is an urban sociologist and works as a senior researcher in the Crime and Security working group at Regioplan Policy Research. She is concerned with subjects such as CCTV, privacy and the police organisation.

Jolanda.Koffijberg@regioplan.nl

Selene Kolman

Selene Kolman is co-founder of Bliin Your-Live and the Nymity Foundation, which does research in the identification aspects of our satellite economy. Kolman studied studied Art History and has a master's degree in Philosophy and in Visual Arts. From 2001 to 2005 she taught at the master's programme New Media and Digital Culture at Utrecht University.

selene@bliin.com

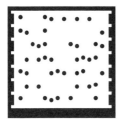

Floortje Daemen

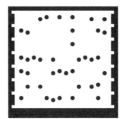

Rinie van Est

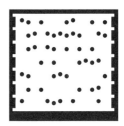

Christian van 't Hof

Bart Schermer

Bart Schermer is a partner at consultancy Considerati. Next to his work at Considerati, he teaches at eLaw@Leiden, Centre for Law in the Information Society at Leiden University. Schermer obtained his doctorate with a thesis on the legal aspects of privacy concerning intelligent software agents.
schermer@considerati.com

Wouter Schilpzand

Wouter Schilpzand is an innovation researcher and advisor at Considerati. He focuses on the social aspects of new technologies. His interests lie especially within the field of Information Society, in which he has spent the past few years trying to understand the social implications.
schilpzand@considerati.com

Ad Schreijenberg

Ad Schreijenberg studied sociology at Tilburg University and administrative and civil law at the University of Amsterdam. Since March 2007 he has worked at Regioplan, researching, amongst other things, audit offices, CCTV, administrative burdens for citizens and organisations, the administration of casinos and the use of the acquis communautaire by migrating families.
Ad.Schreijenberg@regioplan.nl

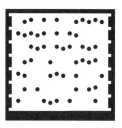

Jolanda Koffijberg

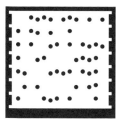

Selene Kolman

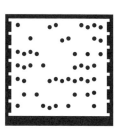

Bart Schermer

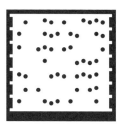

Wouter Schilpzand

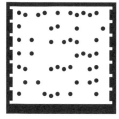

Ad Schreijenberg

Appendix: Technical Terms and Abbreviations

ANPR: Automatic Number Plate Recognition, an optical technology that is used to identify motorists.

Bluetooth: A standard for wireless connections (2.45 GHz) between devices at short distances, in particular mobile phones, headphones and laptops.

GPRS: General Packet Radio Service, an extension to the GSM network for mobile phones that enables a connection with the internet.

GPS: Global Positioning System, a satellite system that helps people to determine their position. The transmitting part of the system consists of 24 satellites that orbit the Earth along six fixed trajectories, each of which emits a unique signal. With reception of at least four of these satellites, a GPS receiver can determine its approximate position on Earth, accurate to within dozens of metres to but a few centimetres.

GSM: Global System for Mobile Communications, the most common standard in the world for mobile phones. Next to exchanging data, this system can also be used for determining where the mobile phone is situated, by looking at which mobile phone towers it logs in.

GSMA: The GSM Association, a worldwide organisation that represents Mobile Network Operators and manufacturers of mobile phones. This is where agreements are made on certain standards.

IP: Internet Protocol, which stands for the way in which computers communicate with each other over networks; this is supported by all computers on the Internet.

IP-address: A unique number given to all computers, so they can be identified within the network. In IPv4 these were roughly 4.2 billion numbers, but they have almost all been used. With the new version, IPv6, a practically infinite amount of addresses are available: 3.4×10^{38}.

Matrix-code: A 2D barcode. Just like barcodes, these codes can be read optically by digital cameras, such as mobile phones. A black dot signifies a '1' and a white dot a '0'; this way a number is shaped which, for example, refers to an internet address. The most well-known examples are the QR Code, Semacode and Microsoft Tags.

MNO: Mobile Network Operator, a business that offers mobile phone services.

NDW: National Data Warehouse for Traffic Information (Nationale Databank Wegverkeersgegevens), a cooperative effort of authorities to collect and use traffic data.

NFC: Near Field Communication, a technology for the quick and wireless transmission of small amounts of data across a very short distance.

PET: Privacy-enhancing technology, a collective term for all sorts of technologies that can be used for the protection of personal data.

PDA: Personal Digital Assistant, a small, portable computer with a network connection.

QR-code: Quick Response code, a matrix-code frequently used in magazines and signposts, to be read with the camera of a mobile phone.

RDW: Government Department of Traffic (Rijksdienst voor het Wegverkeer), an organisation within the Ministry of Transport and Waterworks that registers and controls all vehicles on Dutch roads.

RFID: Radio Frequency IDentification, a technology that consists of chips with antennas that can be read in order to identify products and people.

Router: A device that connects various computer networks and sends data packets from one network to the other.

SE: Secure Element, part of a Near Field Communication application in a mobile phone, in which data can be stored that cannot be changed, such as encryption keys and identification data.

SIM: Subscriber Identity Module, a chip in a mobile phone with which a user gains access to the mobile network. Each SIM card has a unique 13 digit reference number.

Standard: A fixed agreement between technology providers, for example about number systematics or frequencies, in order to allow different devices to communicate with each other.

TLS: Trans Link Systems, the administrative organisation behind the OV-chip card.

TSM: Trusted Service Manager, an intermediary that makes sure that data belonging to various devices, users and providers get exchanged correctly.

UMTS: Universal Mobile Telecommunications System, a set of agreements between providers of various mobile networks and successor to GSM/GPRS. The connecting unit is higher and fewer masts need to be placed.

Wi-Fi: A standard for devices with wireless network connections of 2.4 and 5 GHz. Bandwidth and range are bigger than Bluetooth, as is energy consumption. Frequently used for home networks.

WIMAX: Worldwide Interoperability for Microwave Access, a new standard for devices with wireless network connections of various frequencies. Bandwidth and range are bigger than Wi-Fi and Bluetooth.

Calculation table, from decimal to binary numbers

Decimal	$2^3\ 2^2\ 2^1\ 2^0$	Binary
1	2^0	0001
2	2^1	0010
3	2^1+2^0	0011
4	2^2	0100
5	2^2+2^0	0101
6	2^2+2^1	0110
7	$2^2+2^1+2^0$	0111
8	2^3	1000

Acknowledgements

This book is the result of three years of research and meetings organised by the Rathenau Institute. It started with a sense of urgency that, while almost everyone is on-line, the Information Society is far from coming to a close. Rather, we are entering a new phase: the digitalisation of public space. We observed an increase in devices in the streets that track our behaviour and wondered what this means for us as users of public space.

During the project, we got many good suggestions from our advisory committee: Jos de Haan (SCP, Netherlands Institute for Social Research) and Daniel Tijink (Ministry of Economic Affairs). We also received much expert knowledge on legal matters from Bart Schermer (Considerati) and on technical matters from Jaap Henk Hoepman (Radboud University). Within the institute, Quirine van der Klooster guided our project from the Department of Communications, while Corien Prins and Arre Zuurman took responsibility for this project within the Board of the Rathenau Institute.

On our journey along the many information systems around the world and people who use them, we were helped by many people outside our organisation. Most of them are mentioned in the case studies. Here we would like to emphasise some of them.

Our research in Asia would not have been as fruitful without the support of the Science and Technology officers of the Royal Dutch Embassy. Several visits to Japan were excellently supported by Daan Archer and Kikuo Hayakawa of the embassy in Tokyo. In Seoul, Peter Wijlhuizen helped us out with the South Korean side of our story. Finally, Jaap van Etten of the consulate in Shanghai has been of great help in discovering how the big cities of China are digitalising their public spaces.

The successful collaboration with this network of experts does not end with the publication of this book. Information Technology has a profound influence on the way people live their lives. It has become so common that we tend not to see it anymore. IT has been on our agenda from the start of our institute in 1978 and we will continue to analyse the societal aspects of it.

Frans W.A. Brom
*Head of Technology Assessment,
Rathenau Institute*

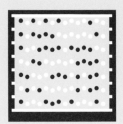

Frans W.A. Brom

Credits

This publication is an initiative of the Rathenau Institute

Editors Christian van 't Hof, Rinie van Est en Floortje Daemen (Rathenau Institute)

Authors Christian van 't Hof, Rinie van Est , Floortje Daemen, Jolanda Koffijberg (Regioplan), Ad Schijenberg (Regioplan), Selene Kolman (Nymity Foundation), Wouter Schipzand (Considerati) en Bart Schermer (Considerati)

Copy editing Isa McKechnie

Design, image concept, illustrations Beukers Scholma

Photography Joyce van Belkom/ HH(=Hollandse Hoogte) p 15; Bram Budel/ HH p 72; Peter Hilz/HH p 44 en p 42; Luuk van der Lee/HH cover; John Schaffer/HH p 47; Solent News&Photo Agency/Rex Feutures/HH p 102; ©iStockphoto.com/ ra-photos p 26; -/Steven Allan p 55

Tags Microsoft Tag

Printing die Keure, Bruges

Paper IJsselprint, 120 gr/m2

Project coordination Marcel Witvoet, NAi Publishers and Quirine van der Klooster, Rathenau Institute

Producer Marcel Witvoet, NAi Publishers

Publisher Eelco van Welie, NAi Uitgevers

NAi Publishers is an internationally orientated publisher specialised in developing, producing and distributing books on architecture, visual arts and related disciplines.
www.naipublishers.nl

Available in North, South and Central America through D.A.P./Distributed Art Publishers Inc, 155 Sixth Avenue 2nd Floor, New York, NY 10013-1507, tel +1 212 627 1999, fax +1 212 627 9484, dap@dapinc.com

Available in the United Kingdom and Ireland through Art Data, 12 Bell Industrial Estate, 50 Cunnington Street, London W4 5HB, tel +44 208 747 1061, fax +44 208 742 2319, orders@artdata.co.uk

Printed and bound in Belgium
ISBN 978-90-5662-808-6

Rathenau Instituut

CHEC

CHEC

KIN

K OUT